WRECKED IN YELLOWSTONE

GREED, OBSESSION, AND THE UNTOLD STORY OF YELLOWSTONE'S MOST INFAMOUS SHIPWRECK

MIKE STARK

RIVERBEND
PUBLISHING

Wrecked in Yellowstone: Greed, Obsession, and the Untold Story of Yellowstone's Most Infamous Shipwreck

Copyright © 2016 Mike Stark

Published by Riverbend Publishing, Helena, Montana

ISBN: 978-1-60639-094-8

Printed in the USA

3 4 5 6 7 8 VP 22

Cover and text design by Sarah Cauble, www.sarahcauble.com

Riverbend Publishing
P.O. Box 5833
Helena, MT 59604
1-866-787-2363
www.riverbendpublishing.com

Front cover photo: The elk-antler-crowned *Zillah* and the larger *E. C. Waters* at the dock on Yellowstone Lake near Lake Hotel, Yellowstone National Park, circa 1906. The steamboats' owner, "Captain" E. C. Waters, stands on the dock. *Courtesy National Park Service, Yellowstone National Park, YELL 206153.*

Back cover photos: Portrait of Ela Collins (E. C.) Waters. *NPS photo.* The wreck of the *E. C. Waters* on Yellowstone Lake's Stevenson Island. *Courtesy of the Yellowstone Gateway Museum of Park County, Montana.*

CONTENTS

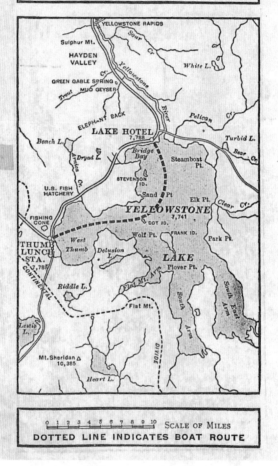

MAP OF YELLOWSTONE LAKE

YELLOWSTONE RAPIDS

Sulphur Mt.

HAYDEN
VALLEY

White L.

GREEN GABLE SPRING
Trout MUD GEYSER

ELEPHANT BACK

LAKE HOTEL
7,788

Beach L.

Dryad L.

Bridge
Bay

Steamboat
Pt.

Turbid L.

Bear

STEVENSON
ID.

U.S. FISH
HATCHERY

Sand Pt

Elk Pt.

Clear

YELLOWSTONE
7,741

DOT ID.

FISHING
CONE

West
Thumb

Wolf Pt.

FRANK ID.

Park Pt.

THUMB
LUNCH
STA.
7,783

Delusion
L.

LAKE

Plover Pt.

CONTINENTAL

Riddle L.

Flat Mt. Arm

South
Arm

South East
Arm

Lewis
L.

Flat Mt.

DIVIDE

Mt. Sheridan
10,385

Heart L.

0 1 2 3 4 5 6 7 8 9 10 SCALE OF MILES

DOTTED LINE INDICATES BOAT ROUTE

*This map shows the boat route between West Thumb and
Lake and was part of an early 1900s advertising brochure by
the Yellowstone Park Boat Company. The brochure boasted:
"Don't, for one minute, think your Yellowstone Park trip
is complete without taking the boat trip across Yellowstone
Lake....if you don't, you'll miss the best part of your Yellowstone Park trip."* COLLECTION OF JOHN ROBINETT.

PROLOGUE

January 1931 and Yellowstone Lake remained ice-bound and forbidding. Three bundled men on the shore pointed their wooden skis south toward a tiny island two miles away and began picking their way across the ice. Yellowstone in winter, as always, was a still and eerie vault that obscured signs of life in hushed banks of snow and bands of rock-hard ice. The noisy summer tourists had long since gone home and the national park was mostly given over to the seventy or so hardy souls who maintained the place along with whatever wildlife figured on eking out a living, whether they were bushy-coated bison, hungry coyotes or waxwings in search of any slim berries still alive. The men on skis, however, were not troubled with survival. They were simply doing what they were told.

Just beyond their view, in the eastern cove of Stevenson Island, lay a once-luxurious steamboat that was now defunct and decaying, tipped on its side and exposed like a prey animal being stripped of its meat. Indeed, by then, many of the ship's steel, wooden and brass parts had been cannibalized.

Salvage crews had also long since carted away the engine, and the giant wood-burning boiler was now being used to heat the nearby Lake Hotel. But most of the carcass of the 125-foot ship—"the finest craft afloat between the Great Lakes and the Puget Sound," it was once called—remained defiantly wedged on the shore of Stevenson Island in the same spot where it had been abandoned years before.

The men, like anyone who had worked on the lake shore, were likely well familiar with the ignominious tales of the ship and its owner: E. C. Waters had been the most hated businessman ever to operate in Yellowstone, dogged by a reputation as a liar, a schemer, a cheat and, by accounts of some of the park's highest officers, utterly insane. He had been arrested, publicly humiliated, investigated by Congress, snubbed by President Theodore Roosevelt, and banned from the world's first national park more than once.

Waters' dream, hatched not long after he arrived in Yellowstone in 1887, had been to ferry thousands of well-off and eager Victorian tourists in high style around the deep blue waters of Yellowstone Lake, the giant expanse of water at the heart of the nation's new park. Yellowstone was becoming a popular destination for a growing class of wealth and privilege in the East keen to see the soaring geysers and strangely colorful hot springs. Trains disgorged them like cattle just a few miles away, and the dudes arrived in the park with money to spend. In those eager and elegant tourists, especially those hoping for a respite on Yellowstone Lake, Waters saw his chance for a cut of the action.

A cunning businessman with formidable political connections, Waters managed to survive for twenty years in Yellowstone, mostly from the profits of running a scrappy steamship called the *Zillah*. But along the way Waters—beset with equal parts ambition, bluster and paranoia—went to war with nearly everyone in Yellowstone who had power and many who did not: military leaders, the railroad, even other entrepreneurs who ran hotels, restaurants and stagecoaches. The darkest turn arrived at the height of his desperation with the suicide of his eighteen-year-old daughter. Stricken and unmoored by grief, Waters blamed her death directly on his enemies in Yellowstone.

With his business in trouble, Waters brought in the pieces for a much larger passenger ship and had it painstakingly built on the shore of Yellowstone Lake. Although it was meant to save himself and replace the struggling *Zillah*, the ship never had a chance to carry a paying customer. Instead it was abandoned on Stevenson Island a few years later, and Waters was left bitter, broken and teetering on financial ruin. It would not be long before he would be kicked out of Yellowstone forever.

By the time the three men skied out to the ship in the winter of 1931, he had long since lost his mind and died hundreds of miles away. The ragged wreck of his starlet steamship on the island, once the object of postcards and breathless news stories, was little more than a destination for drunken parties and curious tourists who had heard the stories of Waters' folly.

"We have people from every state stop and ask about the old boat at the Island," one tour guide, Jack Croney, said of the shipwreck. "Their friends have told them to be sure and don't pass the Lake without first taking a boat over and have the laugh of their lives."[1]

The three men glided across the frozen lake, careful to avoid any weak spots in the ice; January had been warmer than usual and a trip into the water could have deadly consequences. Before long they were on the shore of Stevenson Island, face to face with the wrecked ship. Once the source of so much pride and controversy in Yellowstone, it was nothing but a nuisance now and park rangers had decided it must go.

Daylight dies fast in a Yellowstone winter, so the men went to work, thoroughly dousing the shipwreck with kerosene and setting it aflame.

1 A BOAT IS LAUNCHED

On one of the last Mondays of the summer tourist season in 1905, hundreds of people crowded onto the wooden docks at Yellowstone Lake to witness the christening of a ship. The event had been rescheduled from a few days earlier because of foul weather. It was no matter now. The giant blue lake was calm and placid and perfect, ready to welcome the biggest ship that had ever been deposited on its waters. The crowd, with its back to the yellow-clapboard Lake Hotel, was chipper, dressed for the celebration, and bustling at the event's pomp—even the roses had been shipped nearly two hundred miles from Helena, Montana. E. C. Waters was fifty-six years old and surely buzzing with the kind of electric pride that comes with being at the center of a crowd's attention.

But the occasion rippled with a bittersweet undercurrent. On the dock, twenty-one-year-old Edna Waters stood at the bow of her father's ship, clutching a bouquet of American

Beauty roses and a bottle of champagne. On one sleeve of her yachting dress were emblems of an eagle and an anchor. On the other was an ominous black arm band that matched her black hat and gloves.[1]

Nine months earlier, in the bathroom of the family home in Wisconsin, Edna's eighteen-year-old sister, Anna, had committed suicide by ingesting a cocktail of chloroform and carbolic acid. She had been a literate, pretty society girl who had spent nearly every summer of her life in Yellowstone while her father tended to his boat business at the lake. Her death made all the local papers and badly shook the Waters family, especially her father. E. C. Waters, already weary from two decades at war with the park's military leaders and his business competitors in Yellowstone, said she died because of all those who conspired to destroy him. "It was fear of financial ruin, despondency and humiliation over our business troubles, caused by the indignities, falsehoods and vituperation heaped upon our business in the Yellowstone National Park," Waters fumed a few days after her death.[2]

But here were Waters and his family, a wife and two remaining children, on the shores of Yellowstone Lake, suffering the terrible absence of one of their own and watching as the new steamship absorbed the morning sun. The boat, brought into Yellowstone piece by piece on horse-drawn wagons and carefully assembled on the beach, was finally alive. "We are here to launch the splendid new steamer upon the lake," the emcee, a local newspaper editor, told the crowd. "Not only so but we are here to honor the man who had risked his fortune and who has spent the best years of his life in bettering the conditions of public travel through the greatest collection of natural wonders now upon earth."[3]

A casual visitor to the ceremony that Monday morning

certainly would have left with the notion that Waters was a saint of Yellowstone, or at least one of its noblemen. Waters himself certainly would not have gone out of his way to disavow that perception, and the lengthy speeches on the shore that morning most likely never mentioned his long and tormented history in the park.

Tall, barrel-chested, with heavily lidded eyes and a shock of white hair on his chin, Waters was an impossible figure to miss in the first national park, whether he was stalking the halls of the Lake Hotel or twisting the arms of potential customers while they ate lunch at the lake's West Thumb. He was complicated and smart but carried an air of brittle self-importance. He could be warm, even cordial, but many found him petulant, prickly and unpredictable; solicitous one moment, and a shrill bully the next.

He had, an unhappy visitor once noted, "a most detestable, dishonest face."[4]

Waters had come to Yellowstone in 1887 just as the park's budding tourism industry was catching its stride—but the place was not without controversy. The national park, just fifteen years into its history, had been beset by poachers and vandals under what some saw as feckless bureaucratic management. One year before Waters arrived, Congress called in the U.S. Army to take over.

For those who had to work with Waters in those early days at Yellowstone—especially the army officers charged with maintaining order and overseeing the pleasure of thousands of powerfully well-connected visitors a year—he was a steady irritation and sometimes, because of his political connections, a threat to their careers. He forced one superintendent to be driven out of Yellowstone and tried to frame another to get him fired. His boating customers complained about his shady business practices—overcharging some and sending others onto the lake in creaky, leaky rowboats—while hotel companies complained that he stole their help, bad-mouthed their businesses, and ruthlessly irritated their customers. Still others were sickened by the make-shift zoo he kept on an island where captive elk and bison ate garbage. Over the years, the paper files on Waters at the park's headquarters at Mammoth Hot Springs bulged with complaints, recriminations, unctuous denials, paranoid rants, schemes, investigations, reports and bitter, bad feelings. Waters, one disgusted superintendent said, "has been the source of almost every complaint" in the park.[5]

The man himself, however, was always certain in his victimhood. Waters believed that his troubles in Yellowstone were the result of an unfair system that favored powerful companies like the Northern Pacific Railway and crushed small-time entrepreneurs, himself included, in their path. He became consumed with the idea—it was not altogether wrong—that the game was rigged against him, and that conspiring forces were determined to ruin him not just financially but also personally. The stakes were high in Yellowstone as the railroad company and its influential backers, having made substantial investments into the tourist business in the burgeoning West, sought to secure and exploit a monopoly. They were working hard to establish a network of interconnected profit-generating pieces—railroads, stagecoaches, hotels, and restaurants—and were not about to let Waters gum up their gears.

But in fighting the railroads, Waters became convinced that nearly everyone at Yellowstone was against him, including potential allies in army officers and others trying to run their own business in the park. His "diseased imagination," one fellow entrepreneur in Yellowstone once said, conjured a "hallucination that everyone in the park is trying to rob him."[6]

The speeches being given that Monday morning on the shore of Yellowstone Lake in 1905 never mentioned any of his troubles, of course. This was wholly a celebration of Waters' own making.

When the moment came at 8:45 A.M. to smash the bottle of champagne on the bow, the boat's christened name was notable in part for what it was not. No, the boat would not be named *Anna* after his daughter—even though it probably should have been—nor would it be called *Billings* as previously speculated. It would not even follow the traditional protocol of a female moniker. The name that Edna Waters uttered at the celebration was far more revealing of its owner and chief ambassador. The boat would be called the *E. C. Waters*.

2 TACKING WEST

Before his big ship foundered on Stevenson Island in Yellowstone Lake, before his turbulent decades in Yellowstone, before coming west in restless fit of ambition, Ela Collins Waters was a wild, fidgety, headstrong boy in Wisconsin who observers said "would rather play than study."[1]

His roots ran deep into America's young history. Waters' great-grandfather on his father's side was Judge Jonathan Collins, a sergeant in the Revolutionary War and a major in the War of 1812. His grandfather, David Waters, a builder and a contractor, was also a veteran of the War of 1812. On his mother's side, his great-grandfather was Lt. George Griswold, a soldier in the Revolutionary War. Griswold's granddaughter, Henrietta, was later a political writer, "her contributions to the press being eagerly sought by contending candidates" in her day. Waters' father, Homer Collins Waters, was a farmer and a cattleman born in Fond du Lac, Wisconsin, but raised in Lewis County, N.Y. After marrying Adeline Rockwell, Homer Waters fathered sons Kelsey in 1846, and Ela in 1849. Shortly after Ela was born in Martinsburg, New York, on May 5, 1849, the Waters family moved back to Fond du Lac, which was being overwhelmed with an unprecedented population boom as thousands of easterners moved in to farm, cut timber and take advantage of a new railroad hub that suddenly expanded the marketplace for their goods.[2]

The family settled on a 164-acre farm about four miles outside of town and soon produced three more children: Josephine Arvilla, Emma Augusta and Homer Merton. Homer C. Waters farmed for several more years and then moved into town, where he partnered in a shingle and lumber business. The family grew in prominence and Homer C. even held several public offices in Fond du Lac. But just as the family's fortunes were improving, Homer C. died of "brain fever" in 1858 at the age of thirty-eight. His son Ela was nine years old.[3]

Two years later, Ela's mother married again, this time to a man named William Alsever. That couple had two children: Monroe, who died at age three, and a daughter, Adeline.

Young Ela never took to schooling. "His mind was more on marbles, kite flying, swimming, and raising chickens than on books though he could learn easily enough when he applied his mind to the task. He was very much afraid that something might happen which he would not see. As a boy he was somewhat pugnacious. He was expelled from school many times for these traits."[4]

In the winter of 1863-1864, headmasters kicked Waters out of school yet again. His mind fixated on something more grand and adventurous: joining the military and fighting just as his ancestors had done. That winter, with the Civil War at full pitch, he tried to enlist in the Union Army but was rejected, "chagrined to be apprised of the fact that he was too small in stature and too tender in years to endure the hardships of camp and field."[5]

He returned home in the spring at the age of fourteen and mustered into the Union Army as a drummer boy in Company A of the 38th Regiment of the Wisconsin Volunteer Infantry. Within weeks, his regiment of 913 soldiers shipped out for Virginia. One of the first stops was Cold Harbor, a bloody, lopsided and losing battle against the Confederacy that killed more than 12,000 of Waters' fellow Union soldiers and 4,500 Confederates in thirteen days in June 1864. A lieutenant in Waters' company, A.A. Dye, later described the boy as "an unusually brave and faithful soldier. Although a musician and not required to bear arms, he went into every fight and carried a musket in every engagement in which the regiment participated."[6]

After Cold Harbor, his regiment moved to Petersburg, Virginia, joining the early stages of the siege of Petersburg, a series of trench battles directed by Lt. Gen. Ulysses S. Grant to choke off supplies for Lee's Confederate Army. Waters was at the battle at Fort Stedman in Petersburg, one of the last desperate battles of the war—a fight launched at 4 a.m. with a surprise attack by Confederate troops. "Young Waters got permission of our captain to go to that part of our line, some four miles to our right, and that he carried a gun and fought on the firing line until the fort was captured," Lt. Dye said later. "Though only 14-years of age he did the service of a grown soldier and was always faithful and brave. No one can doubt that he deserves well at the hands of a government he so faithfully served at that trying period."[7]

By the time he mustered out of the Army in July 1865, still just a teenager, Waters had seen profound violence, suffering, death and destruction. No doubt this lingered somewhere inside him for the rest of his life, manifesting perhaps in ways that went unrecognized by even him. But, like many soldiers, his time in the war also became central to his identity for the rest of this life, both as a point of pride and as a witness to the fragile young country that teetered on and survived collapse.

Years later, in a fiery speech to other Civil War veterans, Waters offered a grand biblical vision for the Union Army, saying it "did more for mankind and civilization than any army that history every recorded." The cause put down "a most unholy rebellion, a rebellion that shook the nation from center to circumference, rocking her to and fro." The battles, whose terrible hardships could only be known by those who were there, were fought, Waters said, to "raise the light of day" to "those downtrodden wretches of humanity." In the end, he opined that "the chains that bound four million souls were forever broken."[8]

After the war, young Waters returned home to Wisconsin and attended Ripon College but did not graduate. Instead, he began a restless decade in desperate search to turn a dollar any way he could. He spent a year selling sewing machines. "Made $2,400 and spent $3,200 and was in debt $800 at the end of the year," Waters once told a biographer. "I also bought cattle and sheep, froze them up and shipped them to northern Michigan, and made money."[9]

When he was eighteen, he went to Cheyenne, Wyoming, and quickly fell ill with "mountain fever." Laid up sick and in bed, Waters learned a hard lesson, loaning "a supposed friend from home" all the money he had, $250. The friend "immediately took a train to Frisco and left me there penniless, and I was glad to pawn what I had in order to live until I recovered."

Once he regained his strength, Waters stayed in Wyoming and took a job building snow sheds for the Union Pacific Railroad Company. He made enough to pay back his debts and start looking for new ventures. In the spring of 1869, he set out with 125 other men for the Big Horn Mountains in northern Wyoming. They were chasing "gold by the cartload" and the "Lost Cabin Claim," a long-rumored mother lode of treasure. They did not get far before, as Waters later told the story, they were captured by Indians in the Wind River Valley and held "for some time." The U.S. government eventually brought in troops to drive off the Indians and rescue the mining outfit. Somewhere in the melee, Waters was shot in the leg with a revolver and taken to a hospital in Cheyenne. That ended his adventure in Wyoming. "Finally the bullet was extracted and I returned to Fond du Lac, a poorer but somewhat wiser man," Waters said.

Back in Wisconsin, he settled into a job at a hotel in Beloit ("for the very enticing salary of $16 per month") and let his leg heal. In the last half of 1869, he took a job with the Chicago Board of Trade but that did not last long either. He returned to Wisconsin after receiving word that his stepfather was sick with fever. Back home in Fond du Lac, he spent the next two months caring not only for his stepfather but also for much of the rest of his family as well, all stricken with the same fever. Waters' stepfather, William Alsever, died on New Year's Day 1870—but not before adding to twenty-year-old Waters' burden, giving him care of his half-sister, three-and-a-half year-old Adeline Alsever. "He asked me to care for her and educate her, which I did," Waters said.

His family needed money and so did Waters. He took a job as a traveling salesman selling timber products. The company failed fifteen months later. He finally found steady employment at a New York tea company, pulling in $7,000 to $9,000 a year—far beyond what most Americans were earning at the time. He found love, too. Martha Bustus Amory was "a woman of splendid education, a great reader and a fine musician" and "a favorite in all social circles." They married March 4, 1878, beginning a stable, thirty-one-year partnership that easily mixed family and business. Through the years, Martha acted as Waters' trusted advisor and staunch defender, in some cases, running the Yellowstone boat business on his behalf during his absences.

Waters, however, was restless in the years after they married. Fond du Lac County, which had just 139 people in 1840, was now crowded with more than 50,000 men, women and children. He, like so many, looked to the West, where there were fewer people, more opportunities, and meatier rewards for those willing to take a risk.

The biggest thing going was the Northern Pacific Railway, a massively ambitious project to build a railroad from the Great Lakes to the Pacific Ocean, opening up the entire northern tier of the United States to settlement and, of course, untapped markets for lucrative, industrial-scale logging, farming and mining. Construction started on both ends in 1870. It stalled out during financial crises but, by 1881, the operation was flush with cash and charging ahead at breakneck pace, soon averaging more than a mile of new track every day[10] en route to the spot in central Montana where the two lines would connect. As the railroad pushed farther into undeveloped regions, busy new towns popped up like ant hills, first to feed and house workers and then to act as hubs for the rail service that was soon to follow. Where the rolling plains of eastern Montana Territory gave way to the rugged badlands, on the south bank of the Yellowstone River, Glendive was one of those towns.

The Northern Pacific Railway Company owned most of the town and, directly or indirectly, employed most of its inhabitants. The railroad had picked the spot as a divisional hub for its operations, partly because there was easy access to a steamboat landing on the shores of the Yellowstone River. E. C. Waters, freshly caught up in the railroad fever, arrived in Glendive in 1882. It already had 150 homes, two hotels, a school house, four restaurants, two grocery stores, two butchers, a post office, a baker, a shoemaker and a watchmaker.[11]

After a decade of sleeping in hotels as a traveling salesman, the thirty-three-year-old Waters surveyed Glendive and quickly determined he could find a niche there in the hospitality business. In August 1882, he partnered with the railroad company and a fellow Wisconsin native named Anton Klaus to build and operate a new hotel in Glendive. The deal made sense for Waters—he was joining forces with the most powerful economic operation in the region, riding its coattails into untold opportunities in the opening of the West. He could not then know that the behemoth railroad company would later become a consuming object of his contempt, paranoia, and fear of utter ruination. The three-storey, 60-room Merrill House and livery stable opened in Glendive in the summer of 1882 at a cost of $50,000.[12]

"His ideas gained from experience on the road have been put in practice at the Merrill House, rendering it one of the most pleasant hotels in the Northwest," one account said of Waters. "The equipment of the hotel is first class in every particular and the management is good."[13]

The Merrill House proved lucrative for Waters over the next several years—he apparently even dabbled in philanthropy, donating a 630-pound bell to the Glendive school, which was hung in the schoolhouse tower.[14] He also raised cattle outside of town—his brand was a circle with a "W" inside—and grazed his cows near those owned by Theodore

Roosevelt, who had temporarily abandoned New York politics to come to the Badlands, to escape the grief of his wife's death and try his hand at ranching. Waters bought out his partner, Klaus, in the summer of 1885. By then, Glendive had 1,200 souls and Waters began looking west for a new venture. The logical choice was two hundred miles up the Yellowstone River to the next town, which was then on the cusp of a railroad frenzy.[15]

The Northern Pacific Railway founded Billings as a railroad hub in 1882 (rejecting nearby Coulson, an unruly and often violent settlement whose top lawman was once the legendary mountain man Liver-Eating Johnson). The town, named after Frederick Billings, president of the railroad company, was a primitive affair at first. Indeed in the year it was incorporated, most of its five hundred or so inhabitants were living in canvas tents or covered wagons "waiting for lumber to arrive with which to build houses."[16] Soon enough the railroad company's promises to pour cash into Billings "lit the fuse of a crazed land boom."[17]

The Headquarters Hotel was the first in Billings, initially designed to house engineering crews working on the railroad but later expanded to accommodate the public, many of whom were thankful for such nice service after a days'-long ride from Minnesota or beyond. Waters bought and began running the Headquarters Hotel in 1885 and, by any account, seemed to be successful. The new owner moved to Billings, where he would be an on-again, off-again fixture for decades. His hotels did not fare as well. The Merrill House burned in December 1885 after a fire started in the laundry. Waters vowed to rebuild, with a brick hotel on the same site, but he never did. The Headquarters Hotel in Billings was destroyed by fire six years later.[18]

But Waters, impatient as ever, was already grappling with bigger schemes. In 1886 he was elected to represent Dawson and Yellowstone counties as one of twelve members of the Fifteenth Legislative Assembly of the Montana Territory. It was during his short and fairly uneventful time with the legislature that Waters forged an important friendship with Russell Harrison, son of the future president, Benjamin Harrison.

The younger Harrison had come to Helena a few years earlier, and ran the U.S. Assay Office. Although he did not hold elected office until 1921, Russell Harrison had a way of finding scandal—and sometimes the bizarre. His first big media appearance was just before he came to Montana, representing his family in front of the press in Indiana to announce that the body of his grandfather, son of President William Henry Harrison, had been stolen from its grave "and had just been discovered hanging by the neck in a well at Ohio Medical College, ready for dissection."[19]

When Russell and E. C. Waters met in Helena during the territorial legislature, Harrison was the secretary of the Montana Stock Growers Association, a powerful group of ranchers that held wide sway over regional politics. The two men had more than cattle in common. Both had larger ambitions—Harrison in politics, and Waters in business—and forged a mutually beneficial, sometimes complicated, relationship. Years after they met in Helena, Harrison made sure that Waters, by then a struggling entrepreneur in Yellowstone with a penchant for bending the rules, was shielded from punishment while his father Benjamin was president. As will be seen, the pair got tangled up in a national scandal that spawned a congressional investigation, articles in the *New York Times* and a fair amount of heartburn for those running Yellowstone.

"It was always understood," said one superintendent who battled Waters in Yellowstone during the Harrison administration, "that Waters was under presidential protection."[2]

3 THE STRANGE AND THE SUBLIME

In the summer of 1896, a travel writer and lecturer named John L. Stoddard came to Yellowstone. He was one of 4,659 visitors that year, and took the typical tour that was available, entering through the park's northern entrance near Mammoth Hot Springs, just where the Montana border gave way to Wyoming, and spending several days on bustling, dust-covered stagecoaches and in hotels, sampling alien waters, sniffing the sulfur mud pots and marveling at the thunderous waterfalls along the Yellowstone River. A man in the early stages of a tumultuous religious journey—a born Protestant who attended Yale Divinity School, became an agnostic for more than thirty years, and later converted to Roman Catholicism—Stoddard saw a divine and mysterious hand around every corner in Yellowstone.[1]

"Day after day, yes, hour after hour," Stoddard wrote, "within the girdle of its snow-capped peaks I looked upon a constant series of stupendous sights—a blending of the beautiful and the terrible, the strange and the sublime—which were, moreover, so peculiar that they stand out distinct and different from those of every other portion of our earth."[2]

In some ways, the Yellowstone Stoddard saw was quite like other western landscapes—with its dense conifer forests, cold placid streams, and yawning meadows. But the draw, of course, was Yellowstone's supernatural layer, where mystique braided seamlessly with the ordinary: Forests marvelously pocked with bubbling mud pools and acid geysers; streams lined with yellow, orange and green mats of bacteria, and warmed by super-heated broth from hundreds of feet below the surface. Even the bucolic meadows were interrupted by the nose-curling stench of geological wonders.

Those who arrived in Yellowstone with Stoddard almost always knew what awaited them but came anyway to see for themselves. They arrived with their upscale appetites whetted by newspapers and brochures—magical waters that could heal, a ground that boiled, a raw virgin wilderness that begged to be tamed—and often left as evangelizers of a place that had to be seen and felt to be believed.

Probably stories had been told about the place for at least 10,000 years. Bands of native people passed through Yellowstone time and again, returning to favorite camps and building new ones. They built wickiups, hunted for meat, fashioned tools, fed their families, and buried their dead. Yellowstone was likely most often a spring and summer stop as they gathered supplies and enjoyed long days and chilly nights before traveling on toward winter camps in milder places. Many took pieces of Yellowstone with them, especially tools made from dark volcanic glass chipped away from Obsidian Cliff, an imposing wall of cooled rhyolite lava whose chunks were so valued that they were traded hand-to-hand as far as the Mississippi Valley. Yellowstone, for all its otherworldly mud pots and geysers, was not a fearsome place for Indians, as some of the park's early guides liked to say, but a fruitful and fascinating stop on a never-ending journey for tribes that spanned hundreds of miles in a given year in the American West. White men who later "discovered" Yellowstone often bragged about being the first humans in the region but, in fact, it had been occupied for thousands of years by Native Americans, including the Sheepeaters, Nez Perce, Shoshones, Crows, Bannocks, Blackfeet, and others. The records they left, though, were not on paper but in tools, shelters, burial sites, and oral histories passed from one group to another.[3]

And the geological record of Yellowstone told its own story. It is no accident that one of the first paid explorations here was by a government geologist. Ferdinand Hayden's expedition in the summer of 1871, just ten months before Congress designated Yellowstone as the world's first national park, was designed to return with information "both scientific and practical" from Yellowstone, especially with regard to the region's "geological, mineralogical, zoological, botanical, and agricultural resources."[4]

Ultimately the Hayden expedition's most valuable results may have been the astonishing photos by William Henry Jackson and dreamlike paintings from Thomas Moran— certainly those were what eventually captured the American imagination. Hayden, a former Army surgeon, took a clinical eye to Yellowstone in the hopes of not only confirming wild tales of alien wonders but also of interpreting them through the eyes of emerging geological science.

Yellowstone had long been a place of rumors, speculation and dreams. But even before, it was a place of violence, death and rebirth. Over billions of years it had been, at various times, a barren sand-dune desert, an underwater ocean landscape, a primordial swamp, a desolate plain, well-trodden dinosaur haven, and had seen countless incarnations in-between. The Yellowstone that Hayden saw—including the lake and the park's vast collection of geysers and hot springs—was rooted in the collision of tectonic plates roughly one hundred million years ago. As one massive plate dove beneath another, the land lifted and corrugated mountain ranges bucked up from level ground. Over millions of years, glaciers grew, melted and scoured canyons, while rivers and streams cut a path toward the sea. In what would become the Yellowstone region, volcanoes formed and erupted some fifty million years ago, burying entire forests in ash and sparking the birth of the Absaroka Range, the jagged mountains that still live just east of Yellowstone Lake.

Miles beneath the ground, more trouble was brewing. A churning chamber of molten rock and energy (the same driving modern Yellowstone's geologic wonders) played havoc with the migrating land plates that passed over it. Some twelve million years ago the "hot spot" was beneath what is now southwestern Idaho. It triggered a volcanic eruption so big that the Great Plains were buried in a foot of ash and prehistoric wildlife like rhinos and camels were wiped out by the thousands. Other super-violent eruptions followed, including one 2.1 million years ago, another 1.3 million years ago and yet one more 640,000 years ago that left behind a collapsed volcano that today stretches across forty miles in the middle of the park.

That collapsed volcano, known as the Yellowstone caldera, created a giant bowl that allowed Yellowstone Lake to form and be fed by the headwaters of the Yellowstone River high in the Absaroka Mountains, just southeast of the southern shore. The lake, like a tipping bathtub, drained through an outlet on the northern shore, from where the Yellowstone River beats a rollicking path through the park, out its northern boundary and eventually east to the Missouri and the Mississippi.[5]

After his expedition through Yellowstone in the summer of 1871, Hayden produced a five-hundred-page report of geological observations along with scientific renderings, photos, paintings, and endless musings. It was an attempt to explain this unexplainable place, generate awe and wonder, and ultimately guard it from the voracious profiteers eyeing the West's timber, minerals and other sources of extractive wealth. It had a clear influence on Congress. "The withdrawal of this tract, therefore, from sale or settlement takes nothing from the value of the public domain, and is no pecuniary loss to the government but will be regarded by the entire civilized world as a step of progress and honor to Congress and the nation," said one member of Congress in January 1872 while considering a bill to make Yellowstone the nation's first national park.[6]

The idea for a national park had kicked around for years but an apocryphal version of events eventually took hold, claiming it had been birthed around a campfire near the Firehole and Gibbon rivers during an exploration of the park a year before Hayden. Whatever the case, Hayden's report— with no small help from Jackson's photos and Moran's paintings—finally spurred Congress into action. That, of course, along with the argument from the railroads and others that Yellowstone had no utilitarian purposes, like for growing crops, and therefore its protection was unlikely to rob the potential for those sorts of profits.[7]

On March 1, 1872, President Ulysses S. Grant signed the

"act of dedication" to create Yellowstone National Park. But despite its historic significance, the act passed with little fanfare and unleashed no flood of visitors. In fact, hardly anyone came in the early years after Yellowstone National Park began. The main reason was that it was hard to get to. For the park's first decade, a visit to Yellowstone typically required a rough and long trek on horseback south from a place like Bozeman, Montana, across some 75 miles or so—and that was just to get to see the mystical features at Mammoth Hot Springs. The remaining portions of Yellowstone, sprawling across more than 3,000 square miles, were a daunting prospect, especially because the park was transected by merely a series of bumpy and unpredictable horse paths, with no real roads and few, if any, hospitable places for a meal and a decent night's sleep.

Most of the people who came to Yellowstone early on were curious locals on horseback, though a few rugged souls from beyond made the adventure too. For the first decade, fewer than 1,000 visitors arrived in a typical year. Even the first superintendent, Nathaniel P. Langford, could not be bothered to live there. (That's partly because there was no salary for the job, so he had to keep working as a bank examiner; he visited Yellowstone only three times during his five-year superintendency and issued just one report.)[8]

But where others saw desolation and untamable wilderness in Yellowstone and much of the West, the increasingly powerful railroads and their wealthy benefactors saw an opportunity for profit, subjugation, and expansion. "The untransacted destiny of the American people," the politician and writer William Gilpin had told the U.S. Senate back in 1846, "is to subdue the continent."[9]

Northern Pacific Railway had been chartered by Congress

in 1864 to forge a new line between the Great Lakes and the Pacific Northwest for hauling crops, cattle, timber, and minerals. For their troubles, railroad companies pushing into the frontier were granted ten square miles of land on either side of the track for every mile they built in the West. (This practice, called "checkerboarding," gave the Northern Pacific every other section, or square mile of land, with the public retaining title to the in-between sections. The government then opened public lands to homesteading or held them for Indian reservations.) The railroads ultimately ended up with a combined area larger than Texas—and a fat slice of almost every new business venture in the West that had anything to do with transporting goods back East, which, for years, was pretty much everything the West held. The discovery of gold, silver and other minerals in the American West spurred a furious railroad-building frenzy. Between 1865 and 1920, the number of railroad miles in the U.S. jumped from 37,000 to 253,000. Of course, the railroads were enticed by minerals and the growing prospect of lumber in the West, but they soon discovered one of the most lucrative commodities of all: people with money to spend and a curiosity about the West.[10]

After the interruption of the Civil War, the nation's fitful economy resumed a massive shift from farms to heavy industry and manufacturing, especially in the eastern United States. Congress also subsidized western expansion with laws like the Homestead Act, which gave eager settlers 160 acres of land on the western frontier for $10 and an agreement to farm the land. The revitalized economy, soon humming with eastern factories producing goods and railroads delivering them, helped create a new stratum of wealth in America. Many families, whether they came from old money or were among the newly rich, found themselves with money and time and—after years of soaking in hot baths at resorts in the East only to hear the health benefits were not what had been purported—an emerging inquisitiveness about vacationing in the frontier, whose wild stories were relayed in newspapers and by word of mouth. The railroads, especially in the 1880s, were only happy to oblige this newfound curiosity, dropping their rates for vacationers and building a series of inviting luxury resorts along their routes, including Hotel Del Monte in Monterey, California, the Montezuma in New Mexico and the Antlers Hotel in Colorado Springs, Colorado.[11]

The gambit worked and soon the hotels were cutting handsome profits for the Southern Pacific, Santa Fe, and the Denver and Rio Grande railroads. Why not Yellowstone?

Backers of the Northern Pacific Railway, notably financier Jay Cooke, nursed a long and serious interest in Yellowstone and even helped fund some of the early explorations like the Washburn expedition of 1870. The journeys were among the first to notate the natural wonders of Yellowstone—Old Faithful got its name during the Washburn trip—and helped lay the groundwork for the decision in Congress to protect it as a national park in 1872.[12]

The first step was figuring out how to funnel visitors to Yellowstone. Over the course of just six months in 1883 Northern Pacific built a $1 million, fifty-mile "branch" line from Livingston, Montana, south to the tiny town of Cinnabar, only then being hastily built a few miles north of the park. For decades the line, with its easy curves and moderate grades, was the main arterial track for shuttling eager tourists to and from Yellowstone.[13]

The second step was more complicated: securing a monopolistic network of hotels and stagecoaches in the park. Management of Yellowstone National Park had been placed under the Department of the Interior, an agency with such comically scattered responsibilities—patents, pensions, Indian affairs, even the "Government Hospital for the Insane"—that it was known in the late 1800s as "the Great Miscellany." Disorganized and harried, Interior was an easy mark for meddling and corruption. "The department was a bastion of the spoils system," one historian noted. "Politics permeated its every element."[14]

Although there were some crude concession services early on in Yellowstone, a growing number of wealthy visitors began making noise about the importance of finer hotels, restaurants, and transportation. Yes, they romanticized Yellowstone's wildness but, no, many didn't wish to dwell in the wild themselves, not even temporarily. The upper middle class travelers—"dudes" they were often called—favored posh lodging and sophisticated meals, not canvas tents and meats of questionable origin. The railroad was eager to cater to these well-heeled travelers in Yellowstone, but also cautious about appearances. Railroad companies, once the paragon of American industry, had by then developed a deserved reputation as ruthless, predatory monopolies with an appetite for squeezing out competitors, slashing labor and material costs, and leveraging political power to wring every dollar out of every opportunity. When it came to Yellowstone, the Northern Pacific tried to cloak its influence in hotels and other services, lest it draw the attention of government regulators with some high-minded notion of breaking up companies amassing too much power or profit (years before 1887's Interstate Commerce Act, which attempted to rein in the railroads' monopolistic might). "The methods employed by the railroad company in their approach…were mostly devious, usually camouflaged, so that the corporation's role was more that of a bogey in the shadows than a contestant who could be openly faced," Yellowstone historian Aubrey Haines wrote.[15]

The first public hint of the railroad's financial interest in Yellowstone was in a *New York Times* story in January 1882, announcing the formation of a syndicate "of wealthy gentlemen, more or less intimately connected with the Northern Pacific" who planned "exclusive hotel privileges" in the park, including $150,000 to invest in a 500-room hotel in Yellowstone. On paper it was an easy formula for success: invest in the park's infrastructure, get the government to keep competitors away, and then reap solid profits by selling rooms, food, and transportation to rich people in a remote location with only one proprietor.[16]

These men knew that, by building the branch line to Yellowstone and marketing it to the wealthy and influential, they'd build pressure on the government to get adequate hotels up and running, and fast. It worked, but Interior Secretary Henry M. Teller initially refused to allow a single powerful entity to have a monopoly on the park's guest services. He quickly reconsidered, likely figuring that the only way to get the sort of opulent facilities visitors increasingly demanded required going with a stable, well-financed company motivated to make good on its substantial investment. Besides, dealing with one company, rather than a constellation of big and small players, might make it easier for government administrators in Washington to control how Yellowstone, some 1,700 miles away in the frontier, was managed.

It was more than just an attempt at managerial convenience, though. Teller "knew—and was undoubtedly reminded by [syndicate member Sen. William] Windom and other Northern Pacific lobbyists— that heavy tourist visitation was pending. Nor was he oblivious to the NP's political power in Congress or to the potential repercussions of a failure to have Yellowstone ready for tourists in 1883," one historian has written.[17]

The government soon capitulated. The new syndicate—now known as the Yellowstone Park Improvement Company—would get up to 4,400 acres in Yellowstone, including in some of the most prized locales, like Old Faithful, Grand Canyon of the Yellowstone, and the shores of Yellowstone Lake. The leasing cost was not to exceed $2 per acre, a phenomenal bargain. As part of the "park grab," as it became known, the company was also granted ten years of exclusive rights to operate transportation and retail businesses in Yellowstone, permission to cut trees and mine coal, operate commercial boats on Yellowstone Lake, and even given rights for fruit farms and telegraph lines.[18]

The sweetheart deal—notable even in that era of cozy deals between government and robber barons of industry—was not only a testament to the railroad's influence on the government but also a reflection of the government's understandable inexperience about how a national park should be run. Yellowstone was the first, so it was bound to have some ugly moments.

Fresh with government approvals, the firm's "sly, cunning men" turned to another top investor, notorious Wall Street tycoon Rufus Hatch, for an infusion of cash. Hatch was smooth and ruthless and "at his ebullient, jocular best while gobbling up the weak and unwary of the financial world."[19]

By the summer of 1882, construction had begun on a huge hotel near Mammoth Hot Springs, as workers fed on venison killed in the park and feverishly cut trees in nearby forests for lumber. The project took on a frantic pace as pressure grew to open for the 1883 summer tourist season.[20]

Somehow, they managed to get the National Hotel at Mammoth finished enough to open for business, at least partially. That summer, five thousand visitors (including President Chester Arthur) came to Yellowstone, more than in the previous five years combined. The park, experiencing its first real unveiling to the traveling public, was a hit. "When the European stranger reaches the Mammoth Hot Springs of the Gardiner river he will be more than repaid for having traveled 5,000 miles from England to see them," said one report from the *London Daily Telegraph*.[21]

Not everyone was pleased with the Yellowstone Improvement Company's rapid invasion of Yellowstone. Complaints mounted about the costs and monopolistic nature of the operation. Newspapers ran stories first about Hatch and his profiteering interest in Yellowstone and later about the park's capture by powerful business interests. Even *Harper's Weekly* ran a cartoon, "Desecration of Our National Parks," pointing out Yellowstone's changing character.[22]

"By God," said one rancher north of the park, "they're fixing that thing so that if you want to take whiff of a Park breeze, you will have to pay for the privilege of turning your nose in that direction."[23]

If there was a sunny moment of optimism for the Yellowstone Improvement Company and its influx of tourists in 1883, it was fleeting. Sen. George Vest of Mississippi, who would become one of Yellowstone's fiercest defenders, had learned about the outrageous contract given to the company and set about making it right. Within a year, Vest had reduced the company's leased acres from 4,400 to just 10, and issued a stinging rebuke to those motivated by sheer money when a place like Yellowstone—"a great breathing place for the national lungs," Vest called it—was at stake.[24] The debate over the bill, though, again revealed the enduring opposition to protecting Yellowstone from private market forces attempting to unleash themselves in the West. "The best thing the Government could do with the Yellowstone National Park is to survey it and sell it as other public lands are sold," one senator said.[25]

The Improvement Company soon ran into other, deeper trouble: The recession and financial panic of 1884 hit many of its investors hard, including Rufus Hatch. Banks curtailed loans, capital dried up, despair and doubt set in. In February, the Yellowstone National Park Improvement Company—viewed as such a solid partner by the government just two years earlier—suddenly went bankrupt.

The announcement threw Yellowstone into chaos. At Mammoth, construction on the National Hotel stalled as forty unpaid workers went on strike, and companies complained about $85,000 in unpaid bills for furniture, glassware, carpets, and other materials. The park's superintendent reported widespread "dissatisfaction and resentment" against the company. Confusion and conflict ensued over management of the hotel system as it fell into receivership. The operation limped along during the summers of 1884 and 1885; company officials knew the sweetheart lease in Yellowstone could be lost if services were not provided. Finally, after a series of complicated machinations, a new company emerged to control most of the concession assets.[26]

The irony was that the new Yellowstone Park Association, formed in April 1886, was controlled by some of the most powerful men at the Northern Pacific Railway, the very company that was such a controlling interest in the failed Yellowstone Park Improvement Company. Of the new association's one thousand shares, at least six hundred were owned by top executives at the railroad—it was an ingenious way to direct the Association without violating Northern Pacific's rule against owning any subsidiary businesses. The railroad's influence this time was hardly cloaked—even the meeting to elect the new company's officers was held at the Northern Pacific Railway offices in St. Paul, Minnesota.[27]

At the helm of the new company was Charles Gibson, a starchy sixty-one-year-old St. Louis lawyer and philanthropist who had once been President Lincoln's solicitor general. Gibson had visited Yellowstone in the summer of 1885 and was disgusted by what he'd seen. Hotels had thin, plankboard walls, dismal heating and lighting, and served meats "so tough and mean as to be both unpalatable and indigestible."[28]

The Association was funded with $300,000 in stock purchased by the railroad company and enlivened by a plan to invest in the Yellowstone operations and provide some stability to the park's fledgling tourism business. To do that, they would need someone to manage their hotels, someone experienced and local and ambitious enough to try his hand in the hornet's nest of the world's only national park.[29]

4 WONDERLAND MAN

Word traveled fast in the spring of 1887 that Yellowstone's hotels had a new manager. The owners at the Yellowstone Park Association (and, by extension, the Northern Pacific Railway) had endured several bruising years, including financial collapse and an ugly start to their hospitality business in the new national park. They had invested heavily in catering to Yellowstone's traveling class and now needed to start realizing some profits.

E. C. Waters, by then, had become known in Montana, both as a politician in the Montana territorial legislature and for running the bustling Headquarters Hotel in Billings. He was hired in Yellowstone to manage its five existing hotels plus two more that were planned.

"We have no hesitancy in saying that his eminent capacity to run a hotel will result in greater pleasure and comfort to the traveling public this year than ever before," one Montana newspaper wrote. "The travel to the park this coming season promises to be larger than ever and with half a dozen first class hotels under his charge, Mr. Waters will undoubtedly have a busy season."[1]

He was eager to please his new employers. In some of his first public comments, he toed the Northern Pacific line in publicly complaining that the federal government was not spending enough on improvements at the park. During a visit to the railroad's headquarters in St. Paul, Minnesota, he told a newspaper reporter that most large cities got about $500,000 for maintenance every year, and said Yellowstone was getting just $20,000. "This pittance is merely a waste of money, for nothing of any importance can be accomplished with it," he grumbled, adding that a Russian tourist had already complained to him about conditions at the park.[2]

But the Yellowstone that Waters entered in 1887 was a different place than it had been in the previous decade. Thanks to the railroad, thousands of people were now pouring into the park during the summer, and its managers were ill-prepared to deal with some of the repulsive habits they brought with them, especially wildlife poaching and the destruction of the park's prized geyser cones and hot springs. More often than not, women were fond of breaking off a bit of brittle specimen to take home as a souvenir while the men preferred to scratch their names into the geologic formations. Such bad behavior caught the attention of fellow travelers, including Owen Wister, later famous for writing The Virginian. "Why will people scrawl their silly names on the scenery? Why thus disclose to thousands who will read this evidence that you are a thoughtless ass?" Wister said.[3]

A group of congressmen had come to Yellowstone in 1885 to investigate the bad behavior and found the scant few civilian superintendents, overmatched and underfunded, to be hopeless in the defense of the new national park. "The whole situation was honeycombed with error, corruption, confusion and suspicion," one historian noted. "The Park was in need of redemption; something had to be done."[4]

The U.S. Army took control of the park in August 1886 with the arrival of Company M from the First United States Cavalry from Fort Custer, Montana. The fifty soldiers set up a temporary fort near the base of Mammoth Hot Springs and soon soldiers on horseback were patrolling every road in Yellowstone and inhabiting posts at nearly every point of interest, from Mammoth and Norris to the geyser basin at Old Faithful to Tower Fall and Soda Butte.

They aimed to be an impressive lot. Each reported for duty in a crisp blue uniform outfitted with revolver, cartridge belt, bucket and shovel for fires, well-worn rules and regulations book, and standing instructions to kill wolves and mountain lions, keep people away from grizzly bears and make sure the roads were clear for travelers. The mission was basic: protect Yellowstone and its wildlife and accommodate the growing number of tourists. The arrival of the soldiers was a "pleasing contrast to the ever changing management of blundering, plundering politicians," John Muir once wrote. "The soldiers do their duty so quietly that the traveler is scare aware of their presence."[5]

Camp Sheridan, as the first temporary military outpost was known, became Fort Yellowstone and soon tents became cabins and then cabins became stone buildings and before long it was a proper military settlement with barracks, officers' quarters, a brig, post exchange, pool tables, dance hall and parade grounds. The soldiers had a reputation for being polite but firm, willing to patrol endless months of lonely winters and happy to dance with summer's visiting guests. Many were happy to get Yellowstone duty, while others simply deserted.

The army was still getting settled in Yellowstone when Waters arrived. Although he'd mustered out more than twenty years before, the military has been a regular part of his life as of late. Not long after arriving in Montana, Waters began volunteering with the Grand Army of the Republic, a fraternal organization for Union Army veterans (soldiers of "the late unpleasantness" they were sometimes called) advocating for soldiers, pensions and other services. Waters moved up the Montana ranks—members even wore military-type uniforms—and in late 1886 he was offered a staff job at the national organization then headed by a former Wisconsin governor. In February 1887, at a gathering in Butte, he was appointed chief of Montana's Grand Army of the Republic. (When he stepped down later that year as his attention turned more fully to Yellowstone, Waters named as his replacement his friend, E. C. Culver, who soon followed Waters to Yellowstone and found himself in a bit of trouble.)[6]

Waters, ever proud of his service in the Civil War, joined the soldiers at the first Fourth of July celebration at Camp Sheridan in 1887. "We…gather today to pay our kindly respects to the dear old flag," said Waters. "May it ever be protected in this National Park by as gallant a commander and troops as today are its protectors."[7]

Soon enough he found himself at the wrong end of those "gallant" commanders and troops. In the summer of 1888, while leading a tour near Old Faithful geyser for higher-ups from the railroad company, Waters grew impatient for Beehive geyser to erupt. To speed things along, he resorted to an old trick: tossing in soap to trigger a chemical reaction and induce an eruption—a practice forbidden by the park's military managers. Beehive erupted "grandly" and the visitors erupted in cheers.[8] Waters' hero status proved short-lived. Nearby soldiers arrested him and others in the group, including Thomas Oakes, vice president of the Northern Pacific who would become the company's president just weeks later.[9]

Unfortunately for them, they were all brought before Capt. Moses Harris, the park's first military superintendent. Harris was a no-nonsense Civil War veteran who had won a Congressional Medal of Honor for leading his outnumbered regiment in a rout of Confederate soldiers at Smithfield, West Virginia, in 1864. His three-year rule at Yellowstone brooked few breaches in the rules. "He was vigorous and uncompromising in suppressing lawlessness, just and impartial in his rulings, untiring in his watchfulness for the public interest," wrote Hiram Chittenden, a former Yellowstone engineer turned historian.[10]

The acting superintendent—most of the early military men who first oversaw the park were bestowed that impermanent title—harbored a particular disgust for those who broke or defaced Yellowstone's geological features, especially those who tossed sticks, logs and other objects into the geysers. "Nothing short of the arrest and expulsion from the Park of a number of these offenders, who have the outward appearance of ladies and gentlemen, will probably be effectual to stop the practice," Harris wrote.[11]

True to form, Harris didn't care who the men were that were arrested at Beehive Geyser that day, only that they had broken the law. They were all escorted out of the park to Cinnabar, the terminus of the railroad branch. Somehow Waters kept his job and his $4,000 a year salary.[12]

It was not the first time Harris had expelled Waters from Yellowstone. In September 1887, a newspaper article said Harris had kicked Waters out because Waters "deceived Captain Harris in the matter of the removal of a man named Haraden from superintending the Falls hotel." No other details were provided and it is unclear what became of that order.[13]

But Waters had a way of ingratiating himself in some circles, including with influential newspapermen. Just weeks before the soaping incident, Waters had been in St. Paul, at the railroad headquarters, making himself known, and perhaps inflating his sense of importance among those who didn't know any better: "Col. E. C. Waters, general manager of the Yellowstone Park Association, who has been in the city some days, leaves for his post of duty today," the St. Paul Daily Globe reported on June 6, 1888, likely simply parroting what Waters had said about himself. "It is understood the Old Faithful will outdo himself in honor of his arrival. Col. Waters is deservedly one of the most popular men in Montana and if he would only change his political faith would have the brightest kind of political future."[14]

Later that summer, Waters was involved in a more serious episode involving two of his hotel employees at Mammoth, one named Moore and another called Stivers. One night in early September, Moore was drunk when he "grossly insulted" Dr. Galen Cline, a surgeon working at the fort and living at the National Hotel. Cline punched Moore but the fight was stopped before it could go further. The next morning, Moore and Stivers met Cline as he came out of his hotel room and into the hall and said they were going to "whip him." "He was immediately assaulted by Moore, and a fistfight ensued in the hotel corridor," Harris, the superintendent, wrote later. "Stivers stood by and encouraged Moore and prevented the bystanders from interfering."[15]

The fight eventually broke up and Harris immediately expelled Moore, who had a history of drunken brawling in the park. Harris called on Waters, as manager of hotels, to fire Moore, who worked as a clerk at the hotel. Waters promised to fire him, but then did not do it. Instead, he gave Stivers and Moore work at the tiny town of Cinnabar, just outside the park. Stivers and Moore fumed over the incident and returned night after night to take their revenge on the doctor. A week after the first fight, Cline went into Gardiner to see a patient. Afterward, as he walked toward his buggy, Moore and Stivers confronted him with pistols drawn. As Cline backed up, Stivers knocked him down and began punching him while Moore tried to get a clear shot at the doctor. As bystanders stopped Moore, Cline pulled a pistol from his pocket and fired, hitting Stivers in the groin. Both men were charged. Moore was fined and Stivers was given leniency provided that he leave as soon as possible. The next spring, Stivers told Harris that he wanted to come back to Yellowstone, which Harris took as an indication that Stivers was still after Cline. Harris drew up an expulsion order to keep him out. Waters, though, took the opposite approach. He kicked Dr. Cline out of the National Hotel, claiming that hotel employees had become bitter toward him and that Cline had to leave to avoid "any further trouble."[16]

Waters was apparently still stinging from his embarrassing arrest at Beehive Geyser and could not help taking a bitter stand against the military's approach to the Cline controversy; if Harris took Cline's side, Waters would do the opposite. "It was the slow burn left by this humiliation before his superiors that caused Waters to act as he did in the Cline affair," historian Aubrey Haines later wrote. "Indeed, he was set upon a course of vengeful uncooperation wherever the military was concerned, and this stubbornness led to the ruin of all his enterprises"[17]

Waters' trouble with the authorities only intensified after Moses Harris left his job on June 1, 1889. The next superintendent, Frazier Boutelle, was also a military man and Civil War veteran who quickly got a taste of Waters' shameless tactics. "He began by attempting to get me to go in with him in a scheme of mining coal in the park limits," Boutelle said. "He apparently thought that if he could get me to do something unlawful, he would have me where he could do what he wanted to do afterwards."[18]

Boutelle quickly assessed Waters, saying he was "born a brute" and prone to "infernal cruelty." Since his arrival in Yellowstone, Waters had "bullied everybody, everything, except my predecessor, Captain Harris," Boutelle said. At one point, Waters fired three women working at the Lake Hotel and, knowing they did not have any money and were fifty miles away from help, telegraphed the transportation company and instructed them not to give the women a ride without their paying. He then vowed to charge them $5 a day for each day they remained at Lake.[19]

Boutelle said he never understood how "that scrub Waters" was tolerated in Yellowstone. "Aside from bad business practices, the man was morally rotten," Boutelle wrote years later in a private letter to a subsequent Yellowstone superintendent struggling to deal with Waters. "It was a common practice for him to leave the Mammoth Hot Springs hotel at sun down, en route to one of the hotels, with some poor girl, employed for service, and spend most of the night on the road between the starting point and Norris."[20]

Even the Yellowstone Park Association's own comptroller, who lived for a time on the third floor of the National Hotel, could not stand his co-worker. "The management, or rather mismanagement here is a disgrace to the Association," E. C.

Buchanan said in June 1889. "What Mr. Waters's hold in the Association is I know not—and [could not] care less…the management has a very unsavory reputation and from what has come under my personal notice I think it is deserved."[21]

Despite his reputation, Waters did what he could to keep the Association afloat and ensure the railroad kept a tight hold on Yellowstone profits. Although he would later complain bitterly about the railroad's treatment of his own small independent business, Waters on the railroad's payroll was one of the Association's lead enforcers when it came to driving out competitors. "Gibson and Waters have given me fair notice that they will either buy, scare, or drive us out," said George L. Henderson, a former assistant superintendent in Yellowstone who ran the Cottage Hotel at Mammoth until it was bought out by the Association in 1889.[22]

Around the same time, a newspaper mentioned that Waters had been in Washington, D.C., for two months working on the Association's behalf, "and has presumably fastened a few more rivets in the monopoly the Northern Pacific has on Park travel."[23]

One of Waters' jobs early on was to oversee construction of the new hotel for YPA on the northern edge of Yellowstone Lake, a project that helped sour his reputation as general manager. He insisted on cutting corners by installing the hotel's foundation over an uneven surface of stumps and clay, prompting an inspector to later say there were several places where he could push the foundation over with his foot. He also caught flack for buying cheap furnishings unfit for the Lake Hotel "or any other hotel in the Park for that matter."[24]

Cutting corners may have worked in Billings or Glendive but these were no ordinary Americans that Yellowstone was now catering to. The Northern Pacific's never-ending adver-

tising machine was singing the praises of what it had christened "Wonderland." The target, not surprisingly, was the
powerful, privileged class in the East and Europe, "the most
highly cultured and fastidious people in the world."[25]

Through the ensuing years, thousands of tourists paid
around $50 to spend four or five days touring Yellowstone
on stage coaches, staying in upscale hotels and noshing on
high-class meals. These were business magnates, high-society
families, doctors, judges and politicians who craved novelty
and loathed boredom. They were entitled, demanding and,
at times, repugnant. Rudyard Kipling was a perfect example.
"Today I am in the Yellowstone Park and I wish I were dead,"
Kipling said after arriving on the train in Cinnabar for a trip
through Yellowstone in 1889. "It is not the ghastly vulgar-
ity, the oozing, rampant Bessemer-steel self-sufficiency and
ignorance of the men that revolts me so much as the display
of these same qualities in the women-folk."[26]

One the most popular ways to see the new national park
was the "grand tour," which typically began with a ride on
the Northern Pacific south from Livingston to Cinnabar, a
wind-blown speck of a town at the doorstep of Yellowstone
that was little more than a collection of saloons, a store and
a blacksmith. Getting off the train, visitors were bombarded
by souvenir booths, vendors and come-ons from independent guides offering a tour through "Wonderland." Those
who paid extra for the "grand tour" were whisked onto stagecoaches for an eight-mile ride up to the park's headquarters at
Mammoth. Their arrival created a stir. "The passengers who
alighted from the stagecoaches at the National Hotel and
trooped into the lobby in linen dusters and shaker bonnets
became part of a strange mélange," wrote historian Haines.
"There were businessmen vacationing in black coats and top

hats, smartly dressed ladies, young men in tennis flannels and others in mail-order suits, several ladies in low-cut dresses with flowers in their hair…and a few men in the rough garb of the frontier." [27]

At Mammoth, they could explore travertine terraces and colorful hot pools, buy souvenir spoons, bathe in Bath Lake (often in the buff, but not if women were present), relax on the hotel's sweeping veranda or walk over to F. Jay Haynes' photo shop, tucked neatly behind an impressive fence of elk antlers. Evenings were spent listening to live music in the hotel and hobnobbing with guests from around the world. The next morning, while guests finished their breakfast, a long caravan of stagecoaches queued up along the veranda, most of them yellow, each with four horses, each able to carry eleven passengers. Once fully loaded, they would depart at intervals of five hundred feet or so to keep down the dust. At the helm of the coach was typically a colorful, weather-worn driver (with a name like Big Fred, Society Red or Cryin' Jack) who told stories, and cussed and cajoled his horses along unforgiving roads, hitting every stop along the way. "And so, with a pop of the whip and some warm endearments, such as 'Gid-ap! You pirates!' the lumbering Yellowstone Wagons took their places in the slow moving procession—every tourist filled with a nameless exhilaration, everything especially beautiful, especially marvelous," Haines said. [27]

They would then spend the next several days together, touring the park, eating catered meals in dining tents, singing songs, and sampling every wonder in Yellowstone that was on the 100-plus mile "grand loop" road: Obsidian Cliff, a legendary source of glass-like arrowheads for Indians; Apollinaris Spring, once thought to have mysterious health benefits; and, of course, Old Faithful Geyser. From there it was on to Hayden Valley, a wild assortment of gurgling and foul-smelling springs and mud bogs, and the Grand Canyon of the Yellowstone, where the hotel sometimes included a boisterous brass band and a grizzly bear cub chained to a pole. [27]

"Any intelligent American may thank his stars for anything that will compel him to spend a week in its wonders," said one visitor, James Clarkson, an assistant postmaster general.[28]

Although there were dull stretches—many complained about the endless miles through densely wooded forests — it was more often a heart-strumming trip, exciting, bustling and dirty. And in the middle of the adventure was Yellowstone Lake, a serene redoubt on a mind-bending landscape, a place most visitors were happy to reach and that many were reluctant to leave.

5 WE ARE NOT NAUTICAL MEN

The ink was barely dry on Yellowstone's designation as a national park in 1872 when entrepreneurs begin besieging park managers with their proposals for getting a piece of the action. Leases and applications poured in for hotels, toll roads, stores, guiding services, gardens, newsstands, a sanitarium at Soda Butte Springs and even an ostentatious star-gazing observatory replete with a building "dedicated to the arts, sciences and religion of the future."[1]

At least eight proposals were made to put a passenger steamboat on Yellowstone Lake, some as early as 1879. The following year the park's second superintendent, Philetus W. Norris, endorsed the idea.

It was no wonder that so many gravitated to the lake. It was a vast, stunning and mysterious body of water situated at 7,700 feet above sea level in a depression from a collapsed volcano, the largest high-altitude lake in North America. Twenty miles long, fourteen miles wide and nearly four hundred feet deep, it held an octopus-like shape including two long legs dangling in the south and a bulbous bay known as West Thumb. Despite its frigid temperatures, a series of roiling vents and underwater geysers sprawled along the lake bottom spewing water heated by the huge magma chamber that remains today the engine of all of Yellowstone geothermal wonders. The lake was also a haven for wildlife. Abundant cutthroat trout fed more than forty other animals, including pelicans, bald eagles and grizzly bears. In the winter, though, the lake surface froze into a slab of forbidding ice and snow so thick that that bison, elk and other animals sometimes wandered out to one of the lake's seven islands.

It was the sort of magical place whose reality was so splendid that it easily became the stuff of tall tales. "This is the largest and strangest mountain lake in the world," Legh Freeman, a newspaper editor and publisher, wrote in 1868. "It being sixty by twenty-five miles in size and surrounded by all manner of large game, including an occasional white buffalo that is seen to rush down the perpetual snowy peaks that tower above, and plunge up to its sides into the water. It is filled with fish half as large as a man, some of which have a mouth and horns and skin like a catfish and legs like a lizard....[C]onsidering the surrounding scenery, [it] is the most sublime spot on earth."[2]

Some stories sounded like legends but were not, like tales of Fishing Cone, a bulging geyser on the shore of the lake near West Thumb where fishermen dipped a newly caught trout, still on the line, into the cone's boiling water long enough to kill it and cook it on the spot. Other accounts of the lake simply dripped with awe. "In calm weather, it is a magnificent mirror for the woods and mountains and sky, now pattered with hail and rain, now roughened with sudden storms that send waves to fringe the shores and wash its border of gravel and sand," naturalist John Muir wrote for the *Atlantic Monthly* in 1898.[3]

The lake captivated travelers long before the region became a national park. The oldest archeological sites in Yellowstone are known today to be located along the lake's western shore, where unmistakable evidence shows that native people some 9,000 years ago camped, ate rabbit and bison, scraped animal hides and made tools, probably as a seasonal stop during annual migrations. Sitting on the gravely beach, those people must have been fascinated by the islands in the middle of the enormous blue water. There are archaeological sites on six of Yellowstone Lake's seven islands, including evidence of a prehistoric camp on Dot Island. It is unlikely that visitors swam out to the islands—the water is so cold it can kill within minutes—so it is reasonable to suspect they traveled in canoes, rafts or other types of boats.

That curiosity and fascination was not lost on early white trappers and explorers. A young man from Pennsylvania, Daniel Potts, made it to Yellowstone Lake in 1826, calling it "as clear as crystal" and bordered by geysers shooting water thirty feet into the air. Another traveler, a trapper from Maine named Osborne Russell, described how his party, camping on the lake shore in the summer of 1839, was attacked by Blackfeet Indians. (He was hit in the hip and leg by arrows but survived.)[4]

The 1869 expedition of David Folsom, Charles Cook, and William Peterson—the first organized exploration of the region that would eventually become Yellowstone National Park—took particular note of the lake. The three men spent several weeks wandering the area on horseback. Before heading back north to the Montana Territory, they paused on a hill and took a last wistful look at Yellowstone Lake. "Nestled among the forest-crowned hills which bounded our vision, lay this inland sea, its crystal waves dancing and sparkling in the sunlight as if laughing with joy for their wild freedom," Folsom wrote in his journal. "It is a scene of transcendent beauty which has been viewed by few white men, and we felt glad to have looked upon it before its primeval solitude should be broken by the crowds of pleasure seekers which at no distant day will throng its shores."[5]

A year later, the Washburn expedition traversed much of the lake's shoreline and even attempted to put a boat in the water. "Several islands are seen," wrote Lt. Gustavus C. Doane, the leading U.S. Army officer on the expedition. "These islands doubtless have never been trodden by human footsteps, and still belong to the regions of the unexplored. We built a raft for the purpose of attempting to visit them, but the strong waves of the lake dashed it to pieces in an hour."[6]

The first documented boat on Yellowstone Lake was the *Annie* in late July 1871, built as part of an expedition led by geologist Ferdinand Hayden to explore what would become the national park a year later. The explorers assembled a crude eleven-foot boat out of parts they had packed with them along with a sail cloth and oars carved out of nearby trees. They spent several days sailing the lake, taking depth soundings and exploring islands. The first trip was to an island about a mile and a half from shore. It was later named after James Stevenson, Hayden's loyal and sometimes unpaid assistant and one of the men on the *Annie* that day. "He was undoubtedly the first human that ever set foot upon it," Hayden claimed.[7]

Once the national park was designated and tourists began arriving, many not surprisingly became enamored of Yellowstone Lake. Part of the draw was its notoriously fickle and temperamental waters whose moods were dialed up by the weather: disarmingly placid and blue on some days and, on others, dark, rough and perilous. For some Victorian travelers to whom wild places were becoming less about fear and more about spiritual nourishment, the lake was a sort of salve in an increasingly bleak, dirty, and industrialized world. "To appreciate the beauty of Lake Yellowstone, one must behold it when its waves are radiant with the sunset glow. It is however, not only beautiful, it is mysterious," writer John Stoddard gushed after his 1896 trip. "Around it, in the distance, rise silver crested peaks whose melting snow descends to it in ice cold streams. Still nearer, we behold a girdle of gigantic forests, rarely, if ever, trodden by the foot of man. Oh, the loneliness of this great lake!"[8]

Nathaniel Langford, a member of the Washburn expedition who was later appointed Yellowstone's first superintendent, prized not just the lake's beauty but also its promise that one day its islands would be "adorned with villas and the ornaments of civilized life" so that "the march of civil improvement will reclaim this delightful solitude, and garnish it with all the attractions of cultivated taste and refinement."[9]

One of the first attempts to make money of touring the lake and Yellowstone River by boat was made by T.E. "Billy" Hofer, an early Yellowstone guide. The venture, launched in 1880, was short-lived. "He built a boat and tried to make some money with it in catering to the tourist trade, but did not succeed, and the boat later drifted over the falls," said one report.[10]

The steamboat business on the lake almost got off the ground in 1882 after Gen. James Brisbin, an army officer with political connections in Montana, got permission to ferry park visitors around on a steamer. He estimated the business would be worth $1 million over ten years. The plan died quickly after it became known that the Yellowstone Park Association (YPA), backed by the railroad company, already had a similar right to operate a steamer on the lake. Not eager to compete against one of the richest companies in the country, Brisbin bowed out.[11]

In its early years, YPA showed little enthusiasm for a boat business on the lake. But E. C. Waters, still running the company's hotels in Yellowstone, was often at Yellowstone Lake and undoubtedly saw the magical allure it held for the park's visitors—and its potential for profit. He made his pitch for a boat business not long after Charles Gibson arrived. Waters' initial idea was a "naphtha launch," a small passenger boat popular in the late 1800s in places like the Adirondacks, which ran not on steam but on a fuel similar to gasoline, called naphtha. The more they considered it, the more they realized the naphtha boat probably would not be big enough to handle the number of passengers Waters had in mind.[12]

He wanted something bigger, more worthy of Yellowstone's grandeur and grand visions. Waters' thoughts must have wandered back to his hometown in Wisconsin. *Fond du Lac* translated from French is "foot of the lake," and that town sat at the southern end of Lake Winnebago, where steamboats had been carrying freights and passengers for decades. In Yellowstone, Waters envisioned ferrying passengers from West Thumb to the eighty-room Lake Hotel that was under construction on the northern shore, relieving weary visitors of a twenty-mile stretch of bumpy, dusty stagecoach travel along the park's primitive roads. A couple hours on a boat could do wonders for a weary traveler but Waters would need a vessel capable of carrying one hundred or more people across a sometimes rough stretch of the lake. Gibson, who had a sharp eye for business, bought into Waters' idea. "We are not nautical men, but we want a perfectly safe boat for the tourists," Gibson wrote to the government in 1889.[13]

The endeavor got off to an inauspicious start. Waters went looking for a sturdy steamboat but, given Yellowstone's remote location, the pickings were slim, limited mostly to those running on the Yellowstone River in Montana, which were already spoken for. From there, his choices were either the West Coast, which was more than 500 miles from Yellowstone, or the Great Lakes, which were 900 miles away. Passenger steamboats had been operating on the Great Lakes and surrounding lakes for seventy years, proliferating especially in the 1850s when shipping lines partnered with railroad companies to move their passengers and goods from one end of a lake to another. Waters and Gibson looked to the East for their ship. And yet, even at the Great Lakes, the choices were sparse. The boat they settled on, that would eventually become Yellowstone's famed *Zillah* and carry tens of thousands of passengers over the years, was a pathetic, comically wheezing vessel—once nicknamed Useless—that ran on Lake Minnetonka, just east of Minneapolis.[14]

The boat's origins were in Iowa. It had been built, mostly in Iowa, at a cost of $10,000 for Col. William McCrory, who owned the Minneapolis, Lyndale & Minnetonka Railway Company. At the time, his rail line had just expanded its operations to the small village of Excelsior on the shores of Lake Minnetonka, which was becoming a popular resort destination. McCrory hoped to profit by giving tourists a cleaner, smoother alternative to the horse-drawn carriages that left passengers rattled and coated in a layer of dust. McCrory's boat found trouble early on. As crews were installing the massive, wood-burning boiler in the summer of 1884, it dropped into the lake. Once it was salvaged and installed properly, a trial run in July 1884 revealed two glaring flaws: the boat's three-foot draft was too deep for the shallow uneven contours of Lake Minnetonka and, when the boat neared top speed— said to be a feeble sixteen miles per hour—it listed badly to the starboard side. To boot, its whistle was an obnoxious "ear-piercing shriek."[14]

The boat was never officially christened but soon came to be known around the Minnetonka docks as *McCrory's Folly* and *Useless*. Frustrated and disappointed, McCrory launched the boat anyway. And it did not do badly. Capable of carrying 120 passengers, the *Useless* was larger than many other passenger boats on the lake and thus produced a better business than many of its competitors. "This boat, while she was a dismal failure, seriously interfered with profitable operations of the smaller boats," said the commodore of one competing boat company.[15]

McCrory made a series of repairs and changes, including providing room to accommodate a promenade around the entire boat on the outside of the main cabin. He sold the craft in 1888 to two men who quickly christened it *Clyde* and got rid of that shrill whistle. But, as the lake levels fell, the *Clyde* had an increasingly difficult time finding water deep enough in which to operate.[16]

Waters arrived just in time—at least for the owners of the *Clyde*, who were eager to get it off their books. In the summer of 1889, the Yellowstone Park Association bought the boat for $20,000. In reporting back to Yellowstone's government overseers in Mammoth, Gibson neglected to mention the boat's colorful, if shaky, past. "It was the best boat on the lake," Gibson bragged to Superintendent Boutelle. "It is large enough for the lake and all business likely to be on it, and when you see and try it I have no doubt you will be pleased."[17]

The trick now was getting the steamboat—terribly awkward out of the water at forty tons, 81 feet from bow to stern and fourteen feet across—back to Yellowstone. With a fair amount of effort, workmen cut the *Clyde* into three large pieces on the shore of Lake Minnetonka and loaded it onto railcars. On July 13, 1889, it began making its way to Yellowstone on the Northern Pacific line that ran through Minnesota and Montana and Dakota territories, no doubt stopping in Billings and Glendive—within sight of two of Waters' previous hotels—along the way.

The first 900-plus miles on the train were easy and uneventful. The real work began when the boat arrived at the rail depot at Cinnabar, north of the park's boundary. It would be a complicated journey. Although there's no historical record recounting the details, the boat's massive parts, including the three sections of the steel hull, would have been gingerly hoisted off the rail cars and onto horse-drawn wagons. From there, Waters and Gibson must have known that the rest of the voyage to Yellowstone Lake—across some sixty miles of mountainous, narrow and downright terrifying roads—would be dicey. The route was less a road than a savage pathway cut into the wilderness, with deep dusty ruts, uncertain footing, perilous drop-offs, and stumps sometimes jutting at rude and unexpected angles.

From Gardiner, the caravan would have begun a slow, steady slog uphill toward Mammoth Hot Springs. Off to the west was Electric Peak, an 11,000-foot mountain named during the 1872 Hayden expedition when climbers felt an eerie, crackling sensation as they climbed toward the peak. To the east was the flat-topped Mount Everts, named after the ill-fated traveler Truman Everts, who wandered lost in Yellowstone in 1870 for thirty-seven days before he was rescued at the brink of death. Soon they passed the Boiling River on their left and a spot once called "McGuirk's Medicinal Springs," where rheumatic customers in the 1870s paid to soak in the waters in hope of relief from their disease. Up the road was a 180-degree turn and last arduous climb up a travertine slope to Fort Yellowstone and Mammoth Hot Springs. The steamboat's arrival was certainly a surreal spectacle for the soldiers and visitors at Mammoth, because never before had such a strange caravan passed through the park behind laboring horses. Some had probably heard about the boat's impending arrival—Yellowstone always had a vigorous rumor mill—but, for many present when the boat passed through, it was likely the first time they learned that a full-blown boat-business was starting up at Yellowstone Lake.

From Mammoth, the convoy moved south, directly into the sulfur stench of Mammoth Hot Springs, an otherworldly collection of chalk-white limestone terraces and blue-green pools overflowing with steam and hot spring water. To the right was Mammoth's most famous landmark, Liberty Cap, a 45-foot inverted cone at the base of the terraces that once spewed hot water but which now lay dormant. Then, the horses would have picked their way up another steep incline, around a hairpin turn and past the upper terraces of Mammoth Hot Springs. Not far ahead were the Hoodoos, a mysterious jumble of travertine spires and globular rock piles that adventurers found nearly impossible not to climb and explore.

And, from there, came the most treacherous passage between Mammoth and Yellowstone Lake: Golden Gate at

Kingman's Pass. By then, the horses had pulled Waters' disarticulated boat up some 2,000 vertical feet since taking on their cargo at Cinnabar. Getting through Golden Gate, though, would require more brute strength and more than a little finesse. Kingman's Pass traversed a canyon cut in half by Glen Creek. On one side was an imposing mountain of two-million-year-old volcanic rock. On the other was a heart-stopping drop-off to the craggy canyon bottom. Sandwiched between them was a narrow road and a frightening wooden trestle on the cliff face (bounded by signs on both ends warning ominously: "Golden Gate"/"Walk Your Horses") that had been built a few years before. Passage through the Golden Gate was already a legendary event at Yellowstone, especially for puckered passengers unaccustomed to such perilous travel.[18]

There was a problem when the wagons arrived at Golden Gate. The wide loads could not squeeze through the opening. With little other choice, parts of the rock wall were blasted away, no doubt sending a thunderous shudder through Yellowstone's still, summer landscape. There was another vexing obstacle: the towering column of rock known as the "Pillar of Hercules" that stood like a sentinel in the road, forbidding the steamboat to pass. That too had to be grudgingly moved to the side—and other parts of the road had to be hastily built up in order for the "great weights of the hull" to finally pass over.[19]

All of this trouble could have been eliminated, some joked, if the boat had simply been dipped in Yellowstone's Alum Creek. Legend had it that its mysterious waters could shrink almost anything. One woman, the story went, walked in with size eight shoes and emerged with size ones. Another yarn said a man went through the creek with four huge horses and large wagon and left with four Shetland ponies and a tiny carriage. Alas, the creek was several miles to the south, so it would be no help to Waters and his crew in the pass. [19]

But the hard work of the boat's passing got done, and no doubt more than a few breaths were tensely held as the caravan gingerly made its way through Golden Gate and emerged safely onto Swan Lake Flats, a broad, bucolic expanse of meadows and lakes. From there, it would have been smooth going, as the wagons moved about fifteen more miles south to Norris, a mystical collection of geysers and colorful hot springs and twelve miles east through the forest to the Grand Canyon of the Yellowstone. Another turn, south this time, pointed the caravan another eighteen miles or so, often within sight of the Yellowstone River, through Hayden Valley and past LeHardy's Rapids, where an explorer had nearly died when his raft broke up in 1873. Finally, *finally*, the boat in all its pieces arrived safely on the shore of Yellowstone Lake. "Imagine the labor of conveying such a vessel sixty-five miles, from the railroad to this lake, up an ascent of more than three thousand feet," said one observer. [20]

Waters had a crew at the shore to begin reassembling his new prize, headed up by Amos Shaw, a veteran steamboat pilot from the Great Lakes and the man who would pilot Yellowstone's first-ever steamer. [21] The crew made fast work of the boat, which now included a covered promenade in the bow, inside seating for those looking to escape the elements, and plenty of room on the covered top deck where visitors could wander freely and get an easy look inside the stout pilot house. For Waters, it was surely a proud moment to see the ship's smokestack belch bombastically for the first time into the Yellowstone air as a load of wood inside burned, heating the water in the giant boiler that generated steam to power the vessel. Steamboats were popular throughout much of the United States but this was new in Yellowstone—one of the most remote places in the country.[22]

With a new home, the boat got a new name. Waters, ever eager to ingratiate himself with those in power, rechristened it *Zillah* after the daughter of Northern Pacific president Thomas Oakes, with whom Waters had been arrested after soaping the Beehive Geyser a few years earlier.[23]

The *Zillah* was barely wet before Waters found himself embroiled in another scandal. Just weeks after the *Zillah* arrived, Superintendent Boutelle found out about a poaching scheme by Waters and his pals. E. C. Culver, head of transportation for the Yellowstone Park Association, and R.R. Cummins, YPA's head of construction, had already been expelled from Yellowstone twice. Cummins' recent management of construction of the Canyon Hotel had been deemed "far from satisfactory." Now, guns, traps and a large amount of strychnine—tools of a trade strictly forbidden within Yellowstone's borders since 1886 if not 1883—had been found with the crew that was assembling the *Zillah* on the shores of Yellowstone Lake.[24]

Boutelle accused Cummins of smuggling enough poison into Yellowstone to kill "half the game of the park." Waters had carried Cummins' rifle into Yellowstone in his horse-drawn buggy and thus, per Boutelle, "must have known all about" Cummins' plans to spend the winter staying at Lake and trapping beavers and other fur-bearing animals for money. Waters professed his innocence and claimed Cummins had been framed by a conspiracy. During an investigation, Waters produced for Superintendent Boutelle a witness who said he had heard another man talking in Gardiner, saying Cummins was going to be set up. The witness claimed he did not know Cummins and that he was simply passing along gossip he heard in town. In fact, Boutelle soon learned, the witness had worked for Cummins a year earlier. Waters' attempt to dupe the superintendent thus failed. By the time Boutelle completed his investigation of Waters and his crew, the tourist season in the summer of 1890 was in full swing. The superintendent passed along his findings to top officials at the Interior Department in Washington. He recommended that all three, including Waters, be banned from Yellowstone forever but—in the interest of finishing a smooth tourist season—urged no action until the fall.[25]

Somehow Culver, a friend of Waters' from Billings who had come to Yellowstone with him to join the YPA, managed to keep his job in the park and later became a well-known figure hawking the joys of the national park to tourists riding the Northern Pacific. Waters found himself in a stickier situation. George L. Henderson, the former assistant superintendent and hotelier that Waters and others had squeezed out of business a few years earlier when Waters worked for the Yellowstone Park Association, was now working for YPA as a lobbyist. He was incredulous when he got wind of the poaching scandal. "Can it be possible that Mr. Waters was fooling enough to imperil his own and the company's interest by shipping in arms and traps?" Henderson wrote to Oakes, president of the Northern Pacific, in July 1890. "The [Interior] Secretary is friendly to us, and perhaps the matter can be harmoniously arranged if Mr. Waters acts wisely and discharges those who are inculpated."[26]

Two days later, on July 23, Oakes sent a terse telegram to Waters at his office in Yellowstone: "Important in your own interest that you come at once to Washington. You doubtless know why." Oakes had already made up his mind, telling an associate that he believed Waters broke the law in Yellowstone and that the only reason he had not been expelled was that he managed hotels that were known to be controlled by the powerful and influential railroad. Still, Oakes said, Waters would have to be gone within the year.[27]

Waters, humiliated and bent on revenge, took the train to Washington, D.C., that summer and hatched a plan to enlist his old friend Russell Harrison, whose father, Benjamin Harrison, was now president of the United States. Not only did Waters want to salvage his job in Yellowstone, but he wanted to exact a little vengeance on Boutelle for leveling the poaching charges against him, even though it was probably true. He secured a private meeting with Interior Secretary Noble and emerged confident that "Captain Boutelle would be suspended and would not superintend the park for another year." Sure enough, Boutelle was forced out of his job at Yellowstone less than a year later. (It did not help his case that he had also been complaining about a lack of firefighting resources in the park.)[28] Members of Congress later accused the younger Harrison of political meddling in Boutelle's case, though the full details of his involvement never became public.[29]

During the same week that Waters was in Washington, the Yellowstone poaching scandal hit the front page of *Forest and Stream*, the influential sportsman's magazine edited by staunch Yellowstone defender George Bird Grinnell. The story, under the headline "Unworthy Officials," expressed exasperation that Waters and his crew were not immediately expelled from Yellowstone. "It must be confessed that the prompt ejection from the Park of Waters, Cummins and Culver would have a great moral effect on the general public, and would have mightily increased the public's respect for the regulations for the Park's government," the magazine said.[30] (Cummins would indeed be quickly fired and Waters would eventually be ejected, but Culver would survive to live in Gardiner for many years.)

In Washington, though, Waters worked his political connections, lobbying several members of Congress to put in a good word to keep his job with the Northern Pacific Railway, and several eventually did. He maintained his innocence in the poaching case and vowed that he was the victim of a conspiracy to drive him out of Yellowstone. The railroad did not budge. "He is generally in hot water and I think it better for him to retire from our service," Oakes told a colleague in August 1890.[31]

Oakes fired Waters, mostly because of the poaching scandal and all the headaches and headlines it had produced for the railroad company, but also because he separately had attempted to extort "considerable sums of money" from a meat contractor at the park[32]—an episode that led to Waters' being escorted out of the park by military officials at one point, dropped off at Cinnabar, and told not to return to Yellowstone under penalty of arrest. However, the expulsion did not last.[33]

Tenacious and stubborn and now unemployed, Waters refused to leave Yellowstone. Before he was fired from the Yellowstone Park Association he had shrewdly laid the groundwork for his own new, independent enterprise in the park, the Yellowstone Lake Boat Company. Despite the poaching scandal, Waters' crews in the summer of 1890 had managed to get the *Zillah* assembled, up and running, and happily ferrying passengers between West Thumb and Lake. The steamboat, with a crew of six or seven and capable of carrying 120 passengers, was getting good reviews from visitors. Gibson and the Association showed little interest, though, so Waters made a play to make the business his own, financed with $100,000 of stock, roughly twenty-five percent being owned by himself. During those months when the new boat company was being formed, Yellowstone Superintendent Boutelle confidently warned Waters that Interior Secretary Noble would never approve any new operation in the park where Waters was the president. He urged Waters to reorganize the boat company with "a president of respectable character" at the helm.[34]

Once again, Boutelle lost. On October 11, 1890, Interior Secretary Noble signed a preliminary contract with the Yellowstone Lake Boat Company, E. C. Waters president, to run the *Zillah* on the lake and even to lease some park property along the lake's shore for the operations. The business was finally his.[35]

Back at Mammoth, Captain Boutelle scoffed when he heard the news, and urged Noble to be wary of Waters and his shady ways. "He will be as humble as Uriah Heap & easily controlled," wrote the superintendent, who would soon be expelled from Yellowstone himself.[36]

6 BATTLES BEFORE WAR

Yellowstone has always been a place for predators. The key, of course, is abundant prey. Elk, deer, bison, rabbits, mice—the list of menu items is long and varied. But, when it comes to determining who gets eaten when, there exists a hierarchy. At the top are the most powerful hunters: wolves and grizzly bears. Mountain lions and coyotes follow, and then comes a suite of other predators and scavengers like foxes, ravens, owls, eagles, hawks, and magpies. Everyone eats when there is enough to eat, and meals are often determined by how much prey—which always outnumbers predators—there is to go around. Where the prey roams is often determined by the predators: when wolves move into a valley, the elk disperse to higher ground; when a hungry grizzly shows up in a meadow, pronghorn leave for somewhere else.

The Yellowstone tourist business in Waters' day was not that different from predators and prey. Massive herds of slow-moving tourists migrated in each summer, awash in wealth and unsure of the best way to spend it. The fiercest predators—Northern Pacific Railway and its tentacled enterprises—were deft liberators of cash. Travelers paid to ride their trains across the country (where they were a captive audience for "Wonderland" come-ons) and then paid to stay in their hotels in Yellowstone, eat their food, ride on their stagecoaches and then, happily exhausted and lighter in the wallet, take the train home again.

Waters operated in the shadow of this large-scale predation. No grizzly or wolf, he was more like a tenacious coyote, scavenging profits from the prey that the larger companies had already subdued. It was a complex ecosystem ruled by mega-predators who could change the rules at any time. As in the wild, the bigger eaters were rarely eager to share their score, and their tolerance for competition had a direct correlation to the amount of prey available. In good years, everyone made money. In leaner times, the fight for financial nourishment could be fierce, and men like Waters—hunting alone and competing with other hungry scavengers—had to scrap for their very survival.

Though he scavenged for profits on his own, he was not completely alone in Yellowstone. By 1890, when the *Zillah* started operating, he and Martha had three young children separated by two years each: Edna, Anna, and their youngest, son Amory. The boy had been born in Miles City, Montana, on a spring night in 1888 when Waters and his wife were at a banquet for the Grand Army of the Republic, the service group for Civil War veterans that Waters was heavily involved with. The newspapers reported that Martha gave birth during the event to "a thrifty son." "The occasion was most auspicious and the wine sent down in the banquet hall by the happy father called forth many felicitous expressions for the welfare of the 'kid,'" one report said.[1]

The Waters family spent their summers in Yellowstone, living in what quickly became a dilapidated house next to the Lake Hotel, surrounded by swaying lodgepole pines and a prize view of Yellowstone Lake and the mountains beyond. While Waters was away on the *Zillah*, the family explored the park and viewed all of its wild inhabitants. "The bears are perfectly harmless," Waters told a newspaper reporter in 1891. "Having never been hunted, they have no fear of men. My little daughter, six years old, has sometimes gone within 15 feet of a bear and tossed bits of meat to him."[2]

Those formative years with the boat company were also a period of personal loss for Waters: three of his family members died in quick succession. The first was his younger brother by eight years, Homer, who died in February 1889 in Billings, where he frequently visited Waters. He had been fighting "consumption" for five years. "Cut off in the flower of his manhood, he was but another reminder of the uncertainties of life, and his presence will be missed by all who have been associated with him since his residence here," read his obituary. Waters' mother, Adeline, and his sister Emma died in the first half of 1890. Suddenly Waters found himself, at age forty, without parents and two of his siblings. Nevertheless, he set aside the emotional pain and pressed on with his Yellowstone venture. He became a tireless promoter of his boat company and even of the park itself, though not all of his ideas aligned with the government's plans for Yellowstone.[3]

While staying at the luxury Fifth Avenue Hotel in New York City, Waters told the *New York Times* that Yellowstone could serve as a "zoological gardens" for the rest of the country if only the government would fence in the wild animals and breed them, a suggestion that the park would never consider today and was hesitant to follow even then. There were thousands of elk in the park, he said, and the hundred or so buffalo in Yellowstone—obliterated throughout the West by decades of wanton killing—were in "no danger of becoming an extinct species." He bragged about Yellowstone's unregulated fishing—"Senator Jones of Arkansas landed more than a hundred pounds of trout one day last summer"—and the safety of its wildlife.[4]

Because his old employers at the YPA refused to promote the *Zillah*—he had left a bitter taste in the mouths of too many—Waters had cards printed to advertise to travelers aboard the Northern Pacific. He could not stop himself from taking a jab at those he thought were working against him.

Notice to National Park Travelers

We take this occasion to call your attention to the beauties of Yellowstone Lake, which is the largest body of water in the world for its altitude. It is about 30 miles long and 20 miles wide, and is stated by expert anglers to be the finest trout fishing in the world. Our company has just completed a fine, staunch, and seaworthy steamboat, which is making regular trips for the accommodation of tourists. Said steamer is under the United States inspection laws; thus is perfect in her mechanical structure and operation. The shores of the lake abound with game, which is seen daily from the steamer while upon her regular trips. Herds of buffalo have been seen a number of times at the Thumb of the Lake while tourists were inspecting the beauties and wonders of the Geysers, Paint Pots and Hot Springs. The steamer also lands at the point where one can stand and catch the fish and then cook them in the boiling geyser.

The trip upon the steamer is pronounced by all who have made the same to be the most charming of any in the park. The lake is surrounded by snow-capped mountains, making the scenes terrifically grand; while the only fine accessible view in the park of the Three Tetons is obtained from the decks of the steamer 12 miles from shore. You will find those who will advise you not to go to the lake (perhaps for personal motives) but the universal verdict of all who have seen the lake, fished from her waters, gazed upon the mountains upon her shores, and taken the trip upon the steamboat to the geysers, is that the trip is well worth the time and money expended in the effort. Trusting you will visit the lake during your visit to the Park, we remain.

Yours Very Truly, Yellowstone Lake Boat Company. [5]

Waters' personal anger and potential animosity toward others was clearly evident in this notice, and it did not help his cause with anyone. The YPA saw Waters' card and quickly banned it from Northern Pacific trains until he agreed to remove the parts about "those who will advise you not to go to the lake."[5]

Waters was picking other fights, too. In the summer of 1891, the federal official in charge of inspecting steamboats, John D. Sloan , traveled from Iowa to Yellowstone to inspect the *Zillah*. He arrived later than expected (Waters had delayed the agreed-upon payment for Sloan's travels) and then refused to license the boat because some safety-related repairs were needed. Waters agreed to make the repairs but then went to the president's son, Russell Harrison, to punish Sloan. Soon enough, the steamboat inspector was under federal investigation. "Capt. Waters has considerable influence among a number of Washington city politicians and he doubtless started in to secure Mr. Sloan's scalp," said one newspaper.[6] A subsequent story in another newspaper did not mince words about Russell Harrison's involvement, leading its story: "The scalp of Mr. Sloan of St. Paul, inspector of steamboats, will soon be dangling on Russell B's belt."[6] Sloan's attorney offered a vigorous defense of his client to the press, saying about the required fixes for the *Zillah*: "If there was any error in this regard on the part of Mr. Sloan, it was on the side of public safety."[7] It was probably a testament to park officials' increasing dislike of Waters that Sloan managed to keep his job and, in fact, returned to Yellowstone years later to inspect the *Zillah* again, and the later boat *E. C. Waters*.

Through it all, Waters' steamboat carried on and, despite complaints about the extra $2.50 fee beyond the typical stagecoach-tour costs, gained popularity and became an accepted part of Yellowstone's scenery. By then a long wooden walkway had been built between the lunch station at West Thumb and a dock at the water's edge. At the other end of the trip, riders to Lake Hotel disembarked onto a rough wooden pier, walking past towering stacks of cut wood waiting to feed the ship's boiler. The *Zillah's* meandering two-hour trek, covering about eighteen miles across the lake, "adds much to the pleasure of a trip through the park," said Superintendent George Anderson, who had recently replaced the ousted Boutelle. "It is commodious and comfortable, and I believe perfectly safe." A year later he said the steamer "is greatly enjoyed by all tourists who make the trip on it."[8]

"It was with the greatest interests that I sailed at such a

height on this adventurous craft," John Lawson Stoddard wrote about his trip aboard the *Zillah* on a lake more than 7,000 feet above sea level. "And the next time that I stand upon the summit of Mount Washington, and see the fleecy clouds in the empyrean, one-third of a mile above me, I shall remember that the steamer on Lake Yellowstone sails at precisely the same altitude as that enjoyed by those sun-tinted galleons of the sky."[9]

Indeed Yellowstone's grand lake was gaining a reputation as a place for beauty, serenity, introspection and badly needed respite from the vigors of the park tour. Those staying at the Lake Hotel resort were treated to ample fishing on the shore, hungry grizzly bears putting on a show at the kitchen's back door and more fresh mountain breezes than ever thought possible. And if the lure of the lake and the hotel wasn't enough, a break from the dust proved to be irresistible to many a road traveler. "You either ride in your own dust or in that of the carriages behind you or, if there is a headwind, the dust is driven into your face with a force that blinds and maddens you," George L. Henderson once wrote.[10]

More than 7,000 people visited Yellowstone in 1892, including some fifty members of the Minnesota National Guard's Company D who took a four-hour ride in the *Zillah* on Yellowstone Lake. "Singing and speech-making were freely indulged in, the boys feeling very gay having danced late the night before with some very pretty ladies at a banquet," one report of the boat-trip said.[11]

Emboldened by his growing business venture, Waters floated another idea to the Interior Secretary: Leasing five acres of land along the Yellowstone River to build an elevator from the bank of the river hundreds of feet to the bottom of the Grand Canyon of the Yellowstone River. A man named

D.B. May from Billings had made a similar request earlier that was accepted at first and then, upon better reconsideration, rejected. Waters' elevator proposal never went anywhere either and soon he was preoccupied with more trouble: yet another congressional investigation into his relationship with young Harrison, the president's son.

The controversy went back to 1889 when Waters, still employed at the Yellowstone Park Association, was sent to Washington, D.C., to try to straighten a leasing issue with the government, namely that some of the leases the Association had in the park were not where they wanted to build some of their hotels, including at the Grand Canyon of the Yellowstone. In part it was because of faulty surveying but it was also due to one of the former financiers of the defunct Improvement Company, Carroll T. Hobart, who was secretly conspiring with bureaucrats at Interior to regain some control of Yellowstone land for hotels. "On the one hand, the Superintendent berates us for not erecting a better hotel," the YPA's Charles Gibson had once complained, "and on the other the department declines to relocate the lease to cover the building, and has a rule forbidding any hotels to build until a lease is made for the ground it covers."[12]

Gibson had tried to fix the problem with the Interior Department but failed. Waters suggested that he call upon his friend Russell Harrison, the son of the President, to see if he could influence things at Interior. In return, he would arrange for Harrison to get $5,000 in Yellowstone Park Association stock. "I went to Mr. Harrison and I said...'Mr. Harrison, this company wants to go in and put up their buildings, their hotels, and make some improvements so they can take care of the people....I think it is in the public interest that you ought to try and get this matter fixed up,'" Waters later told a congressional committee, almost certainly offering a sanitized, if embellished, version of events. "Well, he said to me, said he, 'Mr. Waters, if it is for the benefit of the public, and is something that ought to be done, I will speak to the Secretary Noble in regard to the matter.' "[13]

Waters replied that he never told Harrison about the stock reward—it was to be paid out in dividends years later. The only other person who knew about it was Thomas Oakes, the head of Northern Pacific Railway, who said he initially approved of the idea on the wrong assumption that Gibson had also signed off on it. When the Yellowstone Park Association board heard about the arrangement, they immediately voted not to issue the stock to Harrison. The lease issue was also resolved before Harrison could talk to the Interior Secretary.[13]

Nonetheless, Democrats in Congress decided to make political hay out of the arrangement, wrapping it into an investigation of another matter in Yellowstone that involved Harrison and Waters: the ouster of a stagecoach company during Waters' time as the general manager of the Yellowstone Park Association. George Wakefield and his partner, a man named Hoffman, had run a stagecoach service in Yellowstone for years, taking visitors from place to place—all under the auspices of the Yellowstone Park Association's lease with the government. (The YPA got a share of the profits, as did Waters, who owned stock in the transportation operation and once reported a healthy $4,000 dividend.) By almost all accounts, Wakefield's business was good and respectable—even Superintendent Boutelle said it had been "carried nearly to perfection." Suddenly, in the summer of 1890, complaints started rolling in about the transportation business, several anonymous criticisms made the newspapers, and Interior Secretary Noble took a fair share of the blame. Someone also accused Wakefield, a Democrat, of trying to muddle in the recent elections in Montana, an accusation Wakefield called "a damn lie." Nonetheless, the squeeze was on.[14]

In October 1890, Secretary Noble told Wakefield that he needed to cut his ties to the YPA and apply for a lease directly with the government. Noble did not mention that a month earlier a new syndicate had applied to get the same exclusive transportation business in Yellowstone. It was headed up by Silas Huntley, a Montana Republican and good friend of Russell Harrison and members of Montana's congressional delegation, and his backer brother-in-law Harry Child, a banker and budding tycoon out of Helena. Wakefield, desperate to keep his stagecoach business alive in Yellowstone, went to Washington, D.C., with Gibson of the YPA to talk with Noble, explaining that he had worked in Yellowstone for years, poured money into his venture and had a stellar record among visitors. Huntley, on the other hand, had never done anything in Yellowstone. Noble assured the men that Wakefield's business was safe. "Why did he not have the manhood to tell him to his face that he disapproved of his management and desired his dismissal?" Gibson said of the meeting between Noble and Wakefield.[15]

Just weeks later, with no warning, Noble kicked Wakefield out of Yellowstone and gave the lucrative stagecoach franchise to Silas Huntley and Harry Child. Waters helped negotiate the buyout: Wakefield would get about $70,000 for his horses, tack and stagecoaches, even though they were worth about $125,000. The deal left bitter feelings among Wakefield's friends, who felt Harrison and Waters had played a role in driving him out of Yellowstone in order to benefit their well-connected Republican friends Huntley and Child.[16]

Charles Gibson, head of the YPA and a stickler for fairness, complained bitterly about the Wakefield deal, especially coming in such quick succession with Waters' capturing of the boat contract on Yellowstone Lake. "Now, Mr. Huntley and Capt. E. C. Waters, who is the factotum of the boat company, are known all over Montana as the personal, especial, devoted and political champions and friends of the son of the President," Gibson said. "Democrats are kicked out, their rights forfeited and turned over to these two favorite friends of young Mr. Harrison, while their property must be sold at less than half its value to them or be sacrificed outright." Noble claimed that he had not been motivated by politics and personal connections but by a desire to have the best services possible available in Yellowstone, and to have the transportation company responsible directly to the government, not the YPA.[17]

Waters, Oakes, Gibson, and others had been called to Washington, D.C., for a series of hearings in front of Congress on the Harrison scandal. It was a spectacle for the new national park and those called to the Capitol. At one point, a warrant was issued for Waters' arrest because he'd failed to show up to testify. The papers, though, didn't buy the excuse that Waters had fallen ill. Harrison had arrived late the night before, the report went, "it is understood that he and Waters are trying to fix up some kind of story about that stock jobbery which will wash before the committee."[18]

The entire affair was a black eye for Yellowstone, Harrison, the Interior department and Waters, whose testimony during several days of hearings in Congress in the spring of 1892 was termed "evasive" in a *New York Times* story.[19] Waters, wounded by the notoriety, survived the Washington scandal. Back in Yellowstone, though, more storm clouds were gathering.

7   ALL ABOARD

The Harrison scandal did not last long in the newspapers; a larger, more serious crisis was setting in. The panic of 1893, induced partly because railroads had overextended themselves, triggered the worst economic slump the country had seen up to that point. Unemployment soared into the double digits, cash dried up, banks failed and homelessness soared. "Millions feared that in the wreckage of the Gilded Age, democracy itself would crumble," wrote historian Doris Kearns Goodwin.[1] The Northern Pacific Railway, for the second time in its short history, fell into bankruptcy and its problems were compounded by a violent and costly railroad strike in 1894. As the economy soured, fewer people came to Yellowstone—with the number of visitors hitting its lowest in a decade.[2]

"The boat company has suffered quite as much as other industries in the Park from lack of patronage," Capt. George Anderson said.[3] Indeed, during the anemic 1894 summer tourist season, just 973 people rode the *Zillah*—which now sported an enormous rack of elk antlers atop the pilot-house—and revenue became much harder to find. [4] One of

81

Waters' employees, a man named Rapley, who watched over the Yellowstone Lake Boat Company's equipment during the winters, complained to park officials that he wasn't being paid, and disputes erupted over wages for another employee.[5] A third employee, William Boardman, was arrested by park soldiers on suspicion of poaching—he was caught in the park with five beaver traps and two rifles. He was kicked out of Yellowstone and barred from ever returning.[6] (The arrest of another poacher, Ed Howell, caught with the hides of ten buffalo in Hayden Valley, made national headlines and prompted a new law to guard wildlife from illegal kills.)

Waters, though, was preoccupied with how best to weather the faltering economy and tourist declines. He sought permission to build boat landings around the lake shore, including in the lake's far-off Southeast Arm and on several of the islands. He also expanded his operations near the Lake Hotel, renting out fishing boats and tackle (which would become the source of many complaints over the years), and opened up a small grocery store and a blacksmithing service.[7] His boldest proposal, an application to lease land inside Yellowstone to build hotels, was quickly rejected by the government, probably because they did not think he had the money, or the ability, to build and run them.[8]

And then, while spending the winter back home in Fond du Lac, Wisconsin, Waters dreamed up a new scheme, which he outlined in a two-page hand-written letter to Superintendent Anderson, marked "personal" at the top. This novel, if misguided, idea would eventually become a national disgrace and play a role in his demise in Yellowstone. Waters asked if he could set up a private zoo on Dot Island or Stevenson Island for the benefit of his passengers aboard the *Zillah*. "Most everyone who comes to the Park wishes to see wild game," Waters wrote. He offered a long list of possible animals for the island, including elk, moose, antelope, deer, bighorn sheep, bears, foxes and wolves. But it was the bison that would make Waters' island "game show" most famous.

At the time, Yellowstone's wild bison population—like those across the West—was in desperate straits. Some thirty million bison had occupied the Western plains in 1840 but the decades that followed were a wanton orgy of killing spurred by the rise of railroads (including the Northern Pacific) that brought eager hunters by the thousands, some of whom easily killed sixty buffalo in a single day. Millions of bison disappeared from the West in just a few short decades.

Yellowstone was not immune to the slaughter. Just a few hundred remained in the park in 1894, the year Waters proposed his island zoo. Within a few years, the park population dwindled to just two dozen.[9] Waters understood the draw the bison and other animals would have, especially for visitors from the East or Europe who were unaccustomed to seeing any wild animal larger than a deer. Many were also horrified by the slaughter of Western bison and eager to see those rare specimens lucky enough to survive. "I know it would be a source of great pleasure to the traveling public to be able to see such a collection and I cannot see that it would in any way interfere with any other lease holder," Waters told the superintendent in his hand-written letter, studiously avoiding the fact that it would also bring more customers to his boat. "If you approve the above plan write me soon and I will make formal application."[10]

Park officials agreed to allow elk and bison pens on Dot Island, a small outcropping just a half-mile wide near the entrance to West Thumb Bay. They stipulated, though, that the bison had to be imported from outside Yellowstone, lest

they be an unnecessary draw on the park's struggling population. Waters initially secured a deal to buy seven bison from
Chicago's Lincoln Park Zoo for $2,000. He convinced the
Northern Pacific Railway to ship the bison for free from St.
Paul to Cinnabar, the park's railhead just northwest of Gardiner. The deal in Chicago fell through, though, and the bison were resold and shipped to Germany.[11]

Waters quickly brokered another deal, this time with
Charles Goodnight, of the famed Goodnight Ranch in Texas, home to one of the very few remaining bison herds in the
southern United States following the bison massacre in the
plains. On June 21, 1896, four bison (two males and two
females) were loaded onto a boxcar in Texas en route to Yellowstone in the care of a cowboy named William Timmons.
[12] The long journey to Yellowstone included a stop in Waters'
Wisconsin hometown of Fond du Lac, where another female
bison was picked up and an ornery bull from the Goodnight
Ranch was left behind. That "ferocious" 2,200-pound bison
was shot and killed about six months later in Fond du Lac after it became increasingly "violent." About twenty men gathered in a barn to witness the spectacle.[13]

Meanwhile, as the bison train neared Yellowstone, Waters
must have been pleased that rumors were circulating about his
zoo project. "I understand that Col. Waters, President of the
Yellowstone Lake Boat Company, has recently placed on Dot
Island a number of buffalo and wild animals," a Northern
Pacific Railway official wrote to Superintendent Anderson.
"The story is somewhat 'wild' and I am desirous of knowing
just what the facts are."[14]

The bison arrived, later in July, at Cinnabar, where they
were taken off the train and loaded into four horse-drawn
wagons for the sixty-plus-mile trip to Yellowstone Lake.

From there, they were loaded aboard a makeshift barge towed by the *Zillah* and hauled out to corrals on Dot Island. William Timmons, the cowboy from Texas, stayed with them on the island for a month to make sure they adapted to their new home. Dot Island's zoo, which eventually also included elk and bighorn sheep, became a strange but popular tourist destination for years. Waters closed it each fall and the animals were barged back to the mainland and kept near the Lake Hotel for the winter.[15]

Yellowstone's newest gimmick was big news, splashed across the front page of at least one newspaper with the headline, "His New Attraction." "Mr. Waters has invested quite a little money in this undertaking," the story said, "but he figures that in a few years the increase of the herd will net him a handsome return on the investment."[16]

Waters, of course, wanted to push his venture too far. He soon asked the federal government if he could also put Indians, along with one or two tepees or wigwams, on the island each summer so that "tourists might be able to see Indians in their native surroundings." The Secretary of the Interior approved of the exhibit in April 1899, as did the federal Commissioner of Indian Affairs, so long as the Indians "should be entirely willing to go" and that their travel and other expenses to and from Yellowstone were covered. The Indian scheme never came to fruition, probably because Waters either did not have the money for it or did not want to spend it.[17]

As the national economy picked up again, so did visitorship in Yellowstone and business on the *Zillah*. More than 2,500 people rode the steamer in the summer of 1897, a year after the bison arrived on Dot Island, including Col. Samuel Baldwin Marks Young, the park's new superintendent who had just finished as acting superintendent of Yosemite National Park (and who would eventually play a critical role in Waters' final days in Yellowstone). "I made several trips on the boat during the season—one in a severe windstorm—and the boat showed herself to be a staunch craft: every portion appeared neat and clean, the employees respectful, and the master, Mr. E. C. Waters, polite, courteous and obliging," Young said.[18]

A trio of intrepid bicyclists led by Wade Warren Thayer made it as far as the lake shore at West Thumb and was only too happy to continue their adventure on Waters' little ship. "Shortly after noon there came a white dot upon the waters, and presently the little steamer *Zillah* was moored at the landing. It seemed an incongruity in these mountain fastnesses. But we packed up our traps and trundled our wheels aboard, to sail for a delightful, restful afternoon among the bays and islands of this charming lake with the enchanted hills above it," wrote Thayer. "Landing at the great hotel near the outlet we found a little dell nearby where a cool stream trickled, and here we pitched our camp."[19]

For his part, Waters played up the advantages of riding the steamer, including a chance to stretch legs, breathe fresh air and enjoy stunning views of the mountains, forest and glossy blue-green lake—not to mention close encounters with his bison and elk on Dot Island. But, because the steamboat was not part of the ticket that visitors paid to tour the park, it could be difficult to persuade them to pay $2.50 extra to ride it—that was, after all, about half the cost of a night's stay in one of the park's hotels. For those who ponied up, it left an impression. "A party of Philadelphians recently returned from an excursion through Wyoming are still talking about a steamboat ride they enjoyed in Yellowstone lake, which is one mile and a half higher above the sea level than is this city," read one story in the *Philadelphia Record*. "The lake is of clear cold water and well stocked with fish, though 7,740 feet above the Atlantic Ocean. The tiny steamer *Zillah* makes daily runs of 35 miles up and down the lake. Storms that rage with great fury are frequently encountered but the gorgeous sunsets on clear days are greatly admired. Big game is plentiful in that region, and bears and antelopes can frequently be seen from the deck of the steamer."[20]

Although Waters' boat business was tolerated, it was by no means promoted by the powerful corporate interests at Yellowstone Park Association. Waters complained that YPA's employees did all they could to keep travelers off the *Zillah* and that they had opposed his enterprise from the start. Stories spread that the little boat was unsafe or that travelers would be robbed or struck by lightning or drowned or, perhaps a worse sin in the tourism racket, bored. The tactic cut deeply into his profits. "They said almost anything to keep people from patronizing the steamer. Under these conditions, our business was assassinated and ruined," Waters said.[21] He hatched a plan—"to counteract this outrageous and slanderous misrepresentation" and save his company from bankruptcy—to pay stagecoach drivers fifty cents for every tourist persuaded to take the *Zillah*. For a full coachload, that could mean an extra $5.50 for each driver, "a respectable bonus for a man whose wage was $50 per month."[22] "We thought best to pay the drivers a commission for telling the truth about the steamer, the lake, and the beauties of the trip on Yellowstone Lake," Waters said.[23]

Freshly motivated, the stagecoach drivers dutifully steered tourists toward the boat and were happy to get their kickback and, in the process, secure a lighter load for their working horses. It was an amiable, if uneasy, relationship between

Waters and the drivers until it soured in the summer of 1899. Waters was not able to get to Yellowstone until early August that year, so he was not present to pay the fifty-cent kickbacks during the first half of the tourist season—and did not make any arrangements to make sure the payments happened in his absence.[23]

Upset at their lack of commissions, the drivers approached Waters' wife, Martha, who was running the business in Yellowstone while he was away. She denied any knowledge of the commissions and told the drivers to wait until Waters returned. Rather than wait, the drivers launched a revolt of sorts, and thus ignited a new public relations war against the boat company. Whenever a visitor would see the *Zillah* out on the water and ask about it, a driver would say something like, "Oh, they got it back up again!"[24] Drivers also began recirculating their old rumors that the boat was unsafe, that the lake was dangerous and that tourists were apt to be hit by lightning. The ploy worked: Waters estimated he lost $2,000 to $3,000 in business during the boycott. He quickly restarted the kickback program.

Kickback or no, the *Zillah* was becoming part of many Yellowstone travelers' accounts to friends and family back home. "It would be an endless task to attempt to describe the loveliness of this wonderland," Pauline K. Guthrie wrote in a piece published in the *Dubuque Herald* on August 12, 1900, that raved about the hotels, transportation and food during her weeklong tour of the park. "We crossed Yellowstone Lake on the steamer *Zillah* several days ago and the captain very kindly pointed out to us the principal places of interest. We stopped at Elk island, where we saw buffalo, deer and elk roaming about at will. No two by two cage for the small boy to poke peanuts through, but a vast territory, where they can enjoy perfect freedom and roam to and fro in their primitive state."[25]

Waters, Guthrie said, even mentioned that just a few weeks earlier, the *Zillah* had ferried philanthropist Helen Gould, daughter of railroad magnate and robber baron Jay Gould. It was hard to shake the feeling that, as a new century dawned, Waters' venture in Yellowstone might yet succeed.

8   A NEW ENEMY

Captain, soon to be Major, John Pitcher arrived as Yellow-stone's fourteenth superintendent on May 9, 1901. Since George Anderson's departure in June 1897, the superintendent's office had been a revolving cast of restless military bureaucrats, most of whom stayed a year or less before slipping off toward more obscure and probably less interesting assignments. Texas-born Pitcher was forty-six and a veteran of the Nez Perce Indian War of 1877 and the Bannock Indian War of 1878. A graduate of the U.S. Military Academy, he was handy with a rifle and a pistol. Trim and distinguished-looking with a rigid back and bristly mustache, Pitcher became a popular figure at Yellowstone and one of its most recognizable faces, appearing in several photos when his good friend, President Theodore Roosevelt, toured the park two years later. By the time he got to Yellowstone, many of the kinks had been worked out between the army and the businesses who served the tourists. Pitcher was soon enough well-liked by visitors, locals and concession companies and presided over the "golden years of military administration." "While zealously guarding the interests of the park, he never loses sight of the fact that it is the great national playground and that the people have rights here," one local newspaper editor wrote. Another said Pitcher "has the authority of a czar and uses it to so good advantage as to prove the assertion that no government is so good as that administered by a man with supreme authority."[1]

In the years before Pitcher's arrival, E. C. Waters continued to have run-ins with Yellowstone officials. He was arrested in August 1897 for driving his horse-drawn coach at night without permission near Natural Bridge, a place he often took visitors, and a place that he may have used to romance young girls who were not his wife. The following year he was chastised for cutting hay and wood in Yellowstone without authorization. At another point, he was forced to write an eight-page letter answering charges that he had insulted a woman, and he faced more complaints that he was overcharging customers. One of his workers asked military officials for help, saying that he was sixty-six years old and that Waters had left him alone to do work that was too hard and painful, including caring for his boss's cows, sheep, elk and bison.[2]

Within weeks of taking over Yellowstone, Pitcher got sucked into Waters' latest misadventure. In August of 1901, Waters was railing against the army's plans to build a shorter wagon road from the Upper Geyser Basin, where Old Faithful was located, to the Lake Hotel. He claimed Yellowstone's transportation operation, under the control of the still powerful interests at the Northern Pacific, was trying to bypass his stop at West Thumb, the only place where stagecoach passengers caught the *Zillah*. Predictably Waters assumed the road proposal was a direct personal attack but, with President Harrison now out of office, he no longer had a direct connection to the country's top executive. Undeterred, Waters pitched around for a new influential Republican ally and settled on Sen. William B. Allison of Iowa, a man President Harrison once asked to be his Secretary of the Treasury and who, more recently, President McKinley had asked to be Secretary of State. Allison declined both, and remained a U.S. senator. "They are having this road built for the express purpose of ruining the Boat company so they can get our property at their own prices," Waters told the Iowa senator, adding he had "invested all I am worth, and more too, and all Mrs. Waters has" into the company.[3]

Waters took particular aim at the officer in charge of the new road, a West Point graduate turned engineer for the U.S. Army Corps of Engineers named Hiram M. Chittenden, claiming he was owned "body and soul" by the transportation company. Interestingly, Waters also mentioned to Allison that fellow Iowan John D. Sloan—the U.S. steamboat inspector he tried to get fired a decade earlier—can "fully explain to you the situation as he knows it to be."[3]

Waters' complaints about the proposed road, perhaps because of Allison's help, eventually found their way to a top official at the Department of the Interior, who in turn wrote a confidential memo to Pitcher asking for a report on the "truthfulness" of Water's claims, including that Chittenden had an alleged crooked interest in the road. Pitcher wrote back with an attached letter from Chittenden—a highly respected engineer who designed the road system still in use today—about the necessity of the project. The new road will "not interfere in the least with Mr. Waters' business" because coach passengers would still be able to stop at Thumb and get on the *Zillah*, Pitcher said, adding his own support for the road. "Concerning the charges which Mr. Waters has made against the honesty and integrity of Capt. Chittenden...I will simply say that they are absolutely false and that Mr. Waters knew they were false when he made them," Pitcher said.[3]

The new superintendent was also hearing the first of what would be many complaints about Waters' behavior toward Yellowstone travelers. "It has recently been reported to me that you have made yourself exceedingly obnoxious to certain tourists in the park by acting in the capacity of a runner for your boat, at the Thumb Station," Pitcher wrote in a letter to Waters. He also accused Waters of disparaging other transportation companies in Yellowstone to further his own enterprises. "This is not the first report of this kind that has reached this office," bristled Pitcher, "and you are informed that if this matter is reported to me again, the facts will not only be reported to the Secretary of the Interior, but such action will be taken by me to prevent its recurrence."[4]

From his offices near the Lake Hotel, Waters fired back a response, denying Pitcher's accusations, asking for specific names of those he offended and claiming that, despite ten years in Yellowstone, these were first complaints that he was "exceedingly obnoxious." Waters suspected his business rivals in the park, as well as the military, of mounting a campaign against him. "I know it is public talk that certain companies in the Park would do all they could to injure the Boat Company, their business and myself," Waters said. "It is also stated to me by tourists that they came very near not taking the steamer because a soldier had reported that the boat was not safe."[4]

About the same time, the Interior Department in Washington, D.C., secretly launched an investigation of Waters' practices in Yellowstone. "Use discretion about making known the object of your visit to the Park," came the telegrammed instructions to the investigator. Two months later, Special Investigator J.W. Zevely sent a three-page report back to the new Interior Secretary, Ethan Hitchcock, in Washington, D.C., saying that the cost of the two-hour ride on the *Zillah*, now $3, was too high and that row boat rental prices were "very exorbitant." Waters had twelve row boats now and, if anyone wanted to take one of the newer ones out, he required that they take along one of his oarsman, at an extra cost of $1 an hour, according to Zevely's report. Zevely also complained that "Mr. Waters now practically runs a ranch in the Yellowstone Park." Next to the Lake Hotel, he was keeping twenty cows, thirty horses, fifty to seventy head of sheep along with hogs and chickens, just as would be found "on any farm." Just then, park officials were planning renovations to their flagship hotel at Lake. The hotel would be within thirty-five feet of Waters' barns, pigpens, home and other buildings that were, Zevely noted, "unsightly and dangerous." The investigator was one of the first to suggest that a competing boat company be allowed in Yellowstone to squeeze Waters out of business or at least make him straighten up his act. "Unless I have greatly misjudged the situation, his privileges ought to be very greatly limited and the exclusive character of his franchise entirely taken away," Zevely said.[5]

Pitcher reached the same conclusion in his end-of-the-year report to the Interior Department, listing some of the complaints against Waters and suggesting that tourists might be better served if his monopoly on business at the lake was finally broken. The superintendent also noted that while Waters' house was "very neat and pretty," his store was ugly and much too close to where the popular Lake Hotel was expected to expand and that his nearby corrals, full of cows and other livestock, were "filthy and unsightly by their manure." Waters saw the report but refused to take any steps to improve his standing in Yellowstone. He likely believed that would be a capitulation to the enemy, a sign of weakness that would only make him more vulnerable to ruin. Instead, in the manner he had done earlier with Superintendent Boutelle, he initiated an ill-fated campaign to get newcomer Pitcher kicked out of Yellowstone.

A few days before Christmas 1901, Waters was in the New Albemarle Hotel in Livingston, Montana, and started chatting with a newspaperman named E. C. Alderson, who was asking about his business prospects for the next summer. Waters said the outlook was bleak because he now expected his *Zillah* to face competition on the lake and that an officer in Yellowstone was "trying to give him the worst of it." But, "he thought that he knew enough about this officer to have him removed."[6]

Waters then laid out his plan to the newspaperman. He said he had learned that the "officer"—unnamed in the conversation but clearly Pitcher—had been cheating the government by illegally constructing a water line for the transportation company. To make his case, he now needed names of the soldiers who had done the work on the water system so he could turn them against their superior officer. Waters offered Alderson $50 to gather the list of these men's names. Alderson agreed and soon found a soldier in the hotel office who agreed to send him a list of the men for $10. Alderson eventually gave Waters a list of twenty to thirty names and collected his $50 cut. "Alderson felt so good about the matter that he told me all about it," said a bartender at the New Albermarle, J.H. Kane.[6]

Kane initially misunderstood who the "officer" was that Waters was targeting but, when he found out it was Pitcher, he wrote the superintendent a detailed letter about the plot. "Being a man of the world, I don't like to see a good fellow get jobbed," Kane said.[6]

Pitcher had apparently already gotten wind of the scheme and asked Kane whether a man named Botay had been at the New Albemarle at the time. Pitcher was rightfully suspicious. On January 28, 1902, James Breslau Botay, who apparently harbored some of his own crooked connections and may have deserted his military post in Yellowstone (not uncommon during that period), sent a letter to a soldier named Patrick Roberts in Troop G at Mammoth Hot Springs.

> Friend Pat,
> I am still in Livingston and don't know when I will leave. I have been feeling first class and having a good time. I wish you were here. The fellows all think I have gone east so don't say a word to anyone. I want you to do me a favor, go to Cinnabar and make a sworn statement that you worked on that ditch between the Game Corral and the red Transportation stables used by Pitcher. I will send money to Justice of Peace so there won't be any charges against you, you won't regret it. I'll make it worth your while, but whatever you do, don't mention it to anyone.[7]

Meanwhile Pitcher scoffed at Waters' petty accusation. The preceding fall, when Troop F arrived at the military post at the Upper Geyser Basin, Pitcher found that the government horse stalls where he stored a few of his private horses, as well as those owned by the Interior Department, would be needed to accommodate the troop's horses. The Yellowstone Park Association agreed to allow Pitcher to keep his horses elsewhere in a small red barn nearby. In looking at the water supply for the barn, Pitcher realized that it was buried only a few inches below the ground and would almost certainly freeze in the winter. He had a few soldiers and prisoners dig a trench to sink the pipe deeper in the ground. When Waters showed up unexpectedly at the post, apparently in the hopes of blowing the whistle on the project, Pitcher said he was welcome to inspect it and talk to any of his soldiers about it.

Undeterred, Waters contacted higher-ups at the Interior Department to complain about the water pipe. In his defense, Pitcher told the Interior Secretary that Waters "is greatly enraged" about his suggestion to allow competition with the boat business. "I have no fear of Waters so long as he will stick to the truth," Pitcher said, "but from his actions as indicated...I am of the opinion that there is nothing that he would not stoop to."[8]

The war between Pitcher and Waters was just getting started. In 1902, the military office at Mammoth fielded a steady stream of complaints against Waters, his Yellowstone Lake Boat Company, and the *Zillah*. Visitors loved Yellowstone Lake but many could not stand the petty, self-important man who took them out on its waters. One of the first that year came from Pennsylvania State Senator Bayard Henry, who said Waters charged too much (he suggested the steamer ride should cost $1, not $3) and that it was time for a "radical change." "Capt. Waters has had the monopoly of transportation and row-boats on the Yellowstone Lake so long, he seems to forget the fact that the Lake is National property, and does not belong to him," Henry said, adding that the boat operation "is a source of constant irritation and annoyance" and that at least twenty-five people told him the business was a "skin game" "an imposition" and "a fraud."[9]

One visitor, an attorney from Buffalo, N.Y., called the boat ride a "petty swindle"[10] and another said Waters told him not to take the stage ride between the Thumb and the Lake Hotel because it was dusty and bumpy, but the visitor did anyway: "I found the stage ride in distinct contradiction of what Capt. Waters told me."[11]

"This man, 'Captain' Waters as he calls himself," said one traveler, "is a very impertinent and obtrusive person, of whom complaints and criticisms were in the mouths of nearly all persons who came in contact with him on his steamboat and fishing boats while I was there. The general verdict was that he is a public nuisance."[12]

"If this man Waters is not a rogue and a fraud, then the Lord does not write a legible hand, because he has a most detestable, dishonest face," said yet another, who said the boat operation was the only blemish on a perfect trip to Yellowstone. He added that Waters "is perhaps the most unmitigated nuisance that I ever encountered and inflicts himself on all travelers in an odious and unpleasant fashion in obtaining custom for his boat. In addition, he seeks to divert passengers to his boat from the road from the Thumb to the Lake hotel by offering them reductions from his regular fare, and if he cannot get them for one price, takes another."[13]

Waters had his troubles on shore, too. That summer when a horse-drawn wagon lost a load of wood near Thumb Bay, a boy working for Waters suffered a dislocated finger. Waters took the young man over to Lake on the *Zillah* and, before he aimed the steamer back out, told his wife to hitch up their old horse team, Jack and Brownie, so the boy could be taken to the doctor. Another employee, a man named Whitmore, who was driving the wagon when the wood fell out, refused to the let the old team be used, saying they were wild and that he and the boy would be killed before they got to the doctor. One of Waters' daughters hitched up the team and took the young man to see a doctor who was visiting at Canyon. "This Mr. Whitmore went over to the hotel and completed the work of getting intoxicated and went around here making threats against me, claiming he was going to pound me up when I got back," Waters said.

That night, Whitmore went to the boat ccook house, found a carpenter who worked for Waters, and beat him up, blackening both eyes and spraining the man's wrist. He returned to the hotel bar and began spouting about beating up a man named Mr. Nelson, who had hitched up the team for Waters' daughter. The next morning, Waters and the carpenter went to an army sergeant at Lake so Whitmore could be arrested for assault. The sergeant refused, saying that he couldn't arrest him until he heard from his commanding officers—and Whitmore spent the rest of the day threatening Waters and the boat company. "I wish to know for future guidance," a frustrated Waters wrote to Pitcher, "if the laboring men in our employ have any rights in the Park for protection against such abuses."[14]

By now, Waters' bitterness toward Yellowstone's managers had calcified into a brittle fury that was never far from the surface. On a sunny morning in July 1902, Montana's newly appointed, first-ever game warden, W.F. Scott, took passage on the *Zillah* with a few friends. The group was sitting on the deck near the pilot house when Scott mentioned Pitcher's name. Waters overheard and immediately launched a blistering tirade against the superintendent that lasted nearly the entire two-hour trip. Waters, who did not know that Scott and Pitcher were friends, called Pitcher the most-hated superintendent in Yellowstone history, a despot and an abuser of soldiers under his command. Pitcher was cruel to subordinates and soldiers' wives and strong-armed companies he did not like and had aligned himself with the powerful railroad-backed companies that ran the hotels and transportation, Waters said. Scott was shocked by the ship-pilot's frothing accusations. "He said you were doing everything in your power to ruin him," Scott wrote to Pitcher.[15]

As the summer drew to a close, Pitcher and Thomas Ryan, the assistant Interior secretary in Washington, had had enough. Ryan told the top brass at Yellowstone to immediately investigate claims that prices were being changed and that visitors were being over-charged. Those kinds of practices, said the Secretary, reflected badly on Yellowstone and the Interior department and "must be stopped at once."[16]

In a series of acid letters back and forth between park headquarters at Mammoth Hot Springs and boat company offices at Lake, Pitcher laid into Waters, not only about the complaints from visitors (and his bosses at the Interior department) but also about "absolutely false and scurrilous stories" that he told his friend Scott on the *Zillah* in July. "You have been guilty of conduct 'subversive of good order' and are liable to be summarily removed from the Park," Pitcher warned. "If I hear another true report concerning you...I will promptly exercise the authority vested in me as Acting Superintendent of the Park."[17]

A few days later, Pitcher banned Waters from soliciting or in any way presenting his business in tents or buildings operated by the Yellowstone Park Association at Thumb Station and Lake Hotel. "It clearly appears to me that your conduct as a solicitor of business is a source of great annoyance to tourists and that your manners in that connection are obtrusive and impertinent," Pitcher said.[18]

Behind the scenes, Pitcher must have been frustrated with a report by a lieutenant with the 13th Cavalry that month that found no evidence of Waters "having made himself disagreeable." Waters told the lieutenant, who was carrying out the investigation on orders of Interior, that he sometimes gave ministers, children and Army officers reduced rates on the *Zillah* but that otherwise charges were the same for everyone else. The lieutenant verified complaints about fees for fishing boats and tackle.[19]

Waters offered a fiery defense of his character but vigorously ignored the copious, bitter complaints about him filed with the military.[20]

"I know of no case where my language or conduct could in any possible way be construed the above way and for every one that makes such a statement I think I can furnish 100 that will testify that my conduct is not 'impertinent and obtrusive' but rather is kind and considerate," he said. The ban at Thumb and Lake Hotel, Waters said, "will be a great hardship to this company and the traveling public, and you will be assisting the Yellowstone Park Association in their effort, as we believe, to ruin this company[20]

In the winter of 1902-1903, Waters and his family followed their usual practice of returning home to Fond du Lac. After his most brutal summer ever in Yellowstone, he faced a stark choice. It was clear now that the Interior Department and the leaders at Yellowstone, as well as the Yellowstone Park Association, wanted nothing more than to be rid of him and his boat operation forever. If he did not fight back, what were his options?

He had other financial ventures, including stakes in coal mines, hotels and ranching. And just a few years before this, newspapers were reporting about his outlandish scheme, which never materialized, to raise $10 million to buy a half-million sheep and 780 square miles in eastern Montana for a sheep and wool company called the "Montana Consolidated Sheep and Land Company."[21]

But, if the truth be told, most of his money, and indeed his wife's money, was tied up in the Yellowstone Boat Company. Waters, never one to be overly sentimental, also had an emotional attachment to Yellowstone. The park had become a beloved summer home, the place where he and Martha were raising their three children, where they played piano and violin during the cool evenings, where their dog, Major, ran freely in the brisk lake-washed air, and where he had made huge investments into cows, bison, horses, wagons, the blacksmith shop, the grocery, and countless fifty-cent kickback payments to stagecoach drivers. [22]

Walking away now would be a personal disaster. Waters prided himself on his business acumen, and his ability to pull off what others never could, no matter the odds. Thousands of people rode the *Zillah* each summer, and more and more visitors were coming to the park. Some complained about the steamer, sure, but others found great joy in seeing the lake in a way no one else had before. But if he and his enterprise were going to survive and remain in Yellowstone, and weather the storms generated by his hated enemies, his company had to be bigger and more powerful.

Waters' first move was an ostentatious proposal to simply buy the railroad's Yellowstone Park Association, the concessions company that gave him his start in Yellowstone but that he now believed was bent on destroying him. The discussions went further than expected. Twice, Northern Pacific President Charles S. Mellen entertained terms from Waters. But Waters, likely because he could not come up with enough cash, stalled so long that Mellen called off the negotiations, later telling a fellow railroad official he was not ultimately interested in Waters' proposal because of the boatman's sketchy history. "Everyone here and west who knows Waters represents him as utterly unreliable," Mellen said.[23]

Unable to seize control of the most powerful concession operation in Yellowstone, Waters was left with only the boat business. Before long he sent an application to the government to bring a newer, bigger, more glamorous steamboat to Yellowstone Lake. In its own way, it was an act of courage and faith against mounting opposing odds. It was also the only hand he had left to play.

E. C. Waters sits in a rowboat at the mouth of the Yellowstone River in Yellowstone National Park. PHOTOGRAPH BY F. JAY HAYNES. HAYNES FOUNDATION COLLECTION, MONTANA HISTORICAL SOCIETY RESEARCH CENTER PHOTOGRAPH ARCHIVES, HELENA, MT.

Ela Collins (E. C.) Waters arrived in Yellowstone in 1887 and was a notorious fixture in the park for two decades. NPS PHOTO.

Amory Waters, 12, was one of three children born to E. C. and Martha Waters. F. JAY HAYNES' STUDIO, PHOTOGRAPHER UNKNOWN, 1900. HAYNES FOUNDATION COLLECTION, MONTANA HISTORICAL SOCIETY RESEARCH CENTER PHOTOGRAPH ARCHIVES, HELENA, MT.

E. C. Waters strides on the Lake dock beside his steamboat Zillah *in 1904. His home is in the background. The stacked wood powered* Zillah*'s engine.* Photograph by F. Jay Haynes. Haynes Foundation Collection, Montana Historical Society Research Center Photograph Archives, Helena, MT.

E. C. Waters' two-story house was built next to Lake Hotel. Photograph by F. Jay Haynes, ca. 1890. Haynes Foundation Collection, Montana Historical Society Research Center Photograph Archives, Helena, MT.

E. C. Waters (standing far left, in white hat) was the general manager of hotels for the Yellowstone Park Association when officials from the Northern Pacific Railroad visited the park in 1889. Railroad mogul Henry Villard is seated in the center, holding a cane. Photograph by F. Jay Haynes. Haynes Foundation Collection, Montana Historical Society Research Center Photograph Archives, Helena, MT.

Park visitors on stagecoach tours usually stopped at the lunch station at "Thumb of Lake" (West Thumb). This made a captive audience for E. C. Waters to push his steamboat trips. From the J. E. Stimson Collection, Wyoming State Archives, Department of State Parks and Cultural Resources.

The steamboat Zillah *at Lake Dock on Yellowstone Lake, date unknown. The lake's conditions were notoriously fickle.* Photograph by F. Jay Haynes. Haynes Foundation Collection, Montana Historical Society Research Center Photograph Archives, Helena, MT.

In June 1896, the Zillah *pulled a barge containing bison to Dot Island in the middle of Yellowstone Lake. E. C. Waters had bought the bison from the famed Goodnight Ranch in Texas. The corralled bison and elk were a tourist attraction for steamboat passengers but eventually became the source of controversy and disgust.* Stereograph by B. F. Hoyt, ca. 1897, Library of Congress Prints and Photographs Division, Washington, D.C.

In 1889 the steamboat Zillah *was brought from Minnesota in pieces and reassembled on the shore of Yellowstone Lake. It's shown here in 1904 with passengers near Lake Dock.* PHOTOGRAPH BY F. JAY HAYNES. HAYNES FOUNDATION COLLECTION, MONTANA HISTORICAL SOCIETY RESEARCH CENTER PHOTOGRAPH ARCHIVES, HELENA, MT.

Thousands of park visitors rode the Zillah *between 1889 and the early 1900s. This photo shows fifty members of the Minnesota National Guard with the boat in 1893.* PHOTOGRAPH BY F. JAY HAYNES. HAYNES FOUNDATION COLLECTION, MONTANA HISTORICAL SOCIETY RESEARCH CENTER PHOTOGRAPH ARCHIVES, HELENA, MT.

Steamboats, Yellowstone Lake, Yellowstone National Park.

The Zillah *and the larger* E. C. Waters *at the dock near Lake Hotel. E.C. Waters, the man, planned to replace the* Zillah *with his namesake ship, but fate intervened.* Courtesy National Park Service, Yellowstone National Park, YELL 206153.

The Zillah *nears the West Thumb Bay dock with "Captain" E. C. Waters on the bow and tourists on the top deck.* Photograph by F. Jay Haynes, ca. 1890. Haynes Foundation Collection, Montana Historical Society Research Center Photograph Archives, Helena, MT.

A couple walks to the E. C. Waters *at Thumb Dock, 1906. The 125-foot steamboat was painstakingly constructed on the shores of Yellowstone Lake.* STIMSON COLLECTION, WYOMING STATE ARCHIVES, DEPARTMENT OF STATE PARKS AND CULTURAL RESOURCES.

8396.   Steamboat on Lake, Yellowstone National Park.

After E. C. Waters was kicked out of Yellowstone, his grand steamboat was abandoned on Stevenson Island in Yellowstone Lake. COURTESY OF THE YELLOWSTONE GATEWAY MUSEUM OF PARK COUNTY, MONTANA

The E. C. Waters *foundered for years in a cove on Yellowstone Lake's Stevenson Island. In the spring of 1921, wind, waves, and ice heaved the boat onto the beach. Parts of the wreck were removed, including the boiler which was used to heat the Lake Hotel for forty-six years.* Courtesy of the Yellowstone Gateway Museum of Park County, Montana.

The wreck of the E. C. Waters *is still visible on Stevenson Island. Rather than being regarded as an eyesore, the wreck has become an important historical artifact, helping researchers understand some of the earliest years of tourism in Yellowstone.* Mike Stark photo.

9 UNRULY DREAMER

The turn of the century had also been a turning point for visiting Yellowstone. By 1900, word was out that the national park was a must-see destination for tourists heading west. Most of the kinks had been worked out of the hotel and stagecoach systems and travelers could be assured of a safe, sanitized and organized experience—wild but not too wild. Rather than a few thousand visitors every year, it was now ten thousand or more.

For all its draws, Yellowstone remained primarily a playground for the rich and a profit source for railroad backers and their well-connected allies; visitors from more modest economic circumstances were quickly taught their place. "From the time the tourist enters the Park until he leaves, he is constantly impressed with the fact that the affairs of the reservation are being administered for the enrichment of this corporation and the special benefit and convenience of its patrons," said one man of modest means who picked his way through the park on a tandem bicycle. "The great masses of the people—those who cannot afford to patronize this concern—are merely tolerated within the boundaries of the Park."[1] Yellowstone was not yet a democratic place.

Still, the park was featured in newspapers and magazines around the world; it rode a wave of popularity that included Waters' *Zillah* on Yellowstone Lake. During the 1903 season, 13,165 people came to see Yellowstone's wonders. One of them was Hester Henshall, who arrived with her husband, Dr. James Henshall, director of the federal fish hatchery in nearby Bozeman, Montana, and some friends. Her long description is one of the better accounts of a boat trip with E. C. Waters:

> The shrill whistle of the little steamer called us aboard. She is a steel boat, with her name '*Zillah*' on a white flag floating at her masthead. We were soon steaming out into the lake. The Captain's name was Waters, a good name for a steamboat captain. Miss Lillian Ehlert was soon at the wheel steering under the care of the pilot.
>
> Doctor Henshall and Doctor Donaldson and myself sat in the bow of the boat. The scene was beautiful and was all very fascinating to me. Upon the mountains was a vague blue efflorescent haze, like the bloom upon a grape, that made the tint deeper, richer, softer, whether it were the deep blue of the farthest reach of vision, or the somber gray of the nearer mountains, or the densely verdant slopes of the foot-hills that dipped down into the dark shadowy waters of the lake.
>
> Along the western shore was the Absaroka Range of mountains; and in one place was seen the profile of a human face, formed by two peaks of the lofty range. The face is upturned toward the sky and is known as the Giant's Face. It was several minutes before I recognized the resemblance, and then I wondered at my stupidity.

We stopped at Dot Island, a tiny green isle in the middle of the lake, on which are a number of animals, buffalo, elk, deer and antelope. They were fed with hay from the steamboat while we were there. The Captain warned us not to go near, as the big bull buffalo was very fierce. He finally did make a terrific rush and butted the fence until I feared the structure would go down before his fierce onslaughts. He was the last animal fed, and the Doctor said that was the cause of his demonstration; that it was all for effect, and to get us aboard again as the Captain wanted to get the passengers to land at his curio store in season. The man brought another bale of hay and fed the big buffalo, who suddenly became very docile, and we left him quietly munching his hay. I guess the doctor was right.

Soon we were again steaming over the lake. We three again took our places at the bow, and thought it queer that others did not want them. We were told that the '*Zillah*' was brought from Lake Minnetonka, Minnesota, in sections and put together at the lake, which seemed wonderful to me, as she had a steel hull. Too soon our journey was at an end.[2]

The hotel business was changing that summer of 1903. Architect Robert Reamer, a friend of Harry Child, had arrived to build the Old Faithful Inn and begin a massive renovation of the Lake Hotel, including expanding the number of rooms from 80 to 210, extending the roof line and adding its trademark ionic white columns to the front of the building. Although the inn at Old Faithful eventually became the more famous of the two, the Lake Hotel had already become a special pleasure for travelers.

"Guests at Lake Hotel found a serenity absent elsewhere in Wonderland. After a good dinner, well served by waitresses instead of by waiters as at other large hotels in the Park, there were only quiet things to do," historian Aubrey Haines wrote. "Whether one slipped through dim woods behind the hotel, hopeful of seeing bears feeding at the dump, walked the lakeshore, or merely sat and watched the backdrop of wooded hills and rugged peaks far across the water dissolve into the night, the mood was one of restfulness. What a blessing after four days of staging—of sun, wind, dust and mosquitoes!"[3]

Yellowstone National Park had long relied on advertising and word of mouth to bring new visitors—Northern Pacific relentlessly pushed the place to its captive travelers, knowing that most would get there by rail and stay at the hotels closely tied to its own people. But, in the spring of 1903, Yellowstone's best advertisement came with a well-publicized, two-week visit by the most famous outdoorsman in the world, President Theodore Roosevelt.

Roosevelt had been to Yellowstone twice before, but this was his first trip to the park since being thrust into the presidency following the assassination of President William McKinley two years earlier. The President was initially drawn to the prospects of hunting mountain lions in the park but when that did not pan out, he spent a vigorous two weeks hiking, skiing, stalking elk and pronghorn and getting to every corner of the park he could manage. Much of the trip was with John Pitcher, whom he had met twelve years earlier in a snowstorm at Yellowstone and who was now the park's superintendent. "The geysers, the extraordinary hot springs, the lakes, the mountains, the canyons, and cataracts unite to make this region something not wholly to be paralleled elsewhere on the globe," Roosevelt said.[4]

Roosevelt capped his trip back at Gardiner on April 24, 1903, laying the cornerstone of the giant stone arch that would later bear his name and become one of Yellowstone's most recognized landmarks.[4] More than 3,000 people showed up for the ceremony, replete with patriotic bands and "lusting cheering of the assembled multitude," where Roosevelt laid out his vision for the park that called for continued protection of its scenery.[5]

In the audience that day was E. C. Waters, who was stewing over grand plans of his own. After the ceremony, Waters walked over to the tiny newspaper offices of the Gardiner *Wonderland*. With the future of Yellowstone on everyone's lips, Waters could not wait to brag about his next move. "He is having built under special contract in the East an immense schooner for the transportation of passengers across the lake," the newspaper reported a few days later.[6]

Once the new ship was ready, Waters explained to the newspaper, it would begin service on Yellowstone Lake and the *Zillah* would take up new duty, ferrying passengers coming from east of Yellowstone Lake via a new stage coach road under construction about fifty miles west of Cody, Wyoming. He had seen the park's increased popularity, understood the ripple effect that Roosevelt's visit would have on the traveling public, and witnessed first-hand the investment happening at the Lake Hotel. Yellowstone, and especially his little corner of it at the lake, was on the verge of something big. "Colonel Waters' new ship will have a carrying capacity of several hundred people. It will be built in sections and shipped to the Park and there set up ready for business," the newspaper *Wonderland* said. "He has not yet decided upon a name for the boat, but may call it '*The Billings.*' "[6]

First, Waters had more immediate problems to deal with.

A new rivalry was taking shape between himself and Harry Child, the man whom Waters had helped to usher into Yellowstone years before in the ploy to drive out Wakefield and take over the stagecoach business.

Child was born in San Francisco, educated in New England and arrived in the Montana Territory in his early twenties as the mining boom took hold. After running two mines and a smelting operation, he formed a small railroad company in the late 1880s. He also managed a ranch and cattle operations and tried his hand at banking. Child was an ambitious and savvy businessman, who even partnered with Northern Pacific when he could, and who was on his way to a long, lucrative career in Montana's economic frontier. Yellowstone, though, proved too beguiling a temptation to ignore. Like so many others, Child recognized the national park as a cash cow, namely hundreds of rich tourists who were voluntarily captive in a remote and wondrous landscape and wholly dependent on just few concessioners for every one of their basic needs, including food, shelter and transportation.

Child came to Yellowstone in 1890 and never left, spending more than three decades obsessing over the best and most novel ways to wring a profit out of the place. Yes, he loved the park dearly but, first and foremost, it was a stage for doing business and he wanted to command it. "One thing is clear," wrote one historian, "Harry Child wanted to own every hotel, lodge, tent camp, camping outfit, stagecoach line, bus line, livery, grocery, curio store, photo shop, garage and gas station in the park."[7]

Child became a titan in Yellowstone, likely its most powerful and influential businessman as the park underwent a bumpy transition from primitive park in the late 1800s to a slick experience catering to a new class of automobile travelers in the early twentieth century. Though he was noted for his visionary approach to tourism, Child developed a reputation as "utterly ruthless" and a "typical robber baron," according to one superintendent. "If Harry Child died and appeared at the Pearly Gates, and St. Peter suggested they flip a coin to see if he would enter Heaven or Hell," said Jack Ellis Haynes, a fellow businessman in Yellowstone, "Harry would have agreed. Then he would have caught the coin in mid-air and run away with it."[7]

Although Child arrived in Yellowstone with his stagecoach business after the Wakefield debacle, he could not be satisfied with such a small slice of the action. Five-foot-five and a little tubby, Child longed to be a giant of Yellowstone. One of his biggest breaks came after Waters' failed attempt to buy the Yellowstone Park Association (YPA). Once that fell through, the company was sold to Child and his brothers-in-law, Silas Huntley and Edmund W. Bach. The Northern Pacific kept its tentacles on the company, though. The deal to buy the YPA was financed with a loan from a subsidiary of the railroad company. And when Child, who became president of the YPA, was short on cash to build new hotels or make improvements, it was the railroad who stepped in with its finances. Child and the railroad would be intimately linked for decades in Yellowstone, a relationship that benefited both financially. "His motto was never to be in debt to a railroad for less than a million dollars," Horace Albright, the former Yellowstone superintendent and National Park Service director, once said.[7]

That cozy relationship never ceased to irritate Waters. More than once Waters raised legitimate concerns about a monopoly in Yellowstone, recognizing that the railroad still pulled the strings on business in the park even after the as-

sociation had been sold. By 1903 Waters had stopped paying the fifty-cent kickback to stagecoach drivers of the Yellowstone Park Association. A year earlier, he had reached an
agreement with Child. Child's company agreed to make the
ride on the *Zillah* part of its tour package in the hopes that it
would eliminate complaints about Waters' obnoxious efforts
to induce riders for his boat. Customers would also no longer
have to pay the additional fee to ride the boat. In exchange,
Waters agreed to remove "unsightly" buildings and corrals
next to the Lake Hotel—and not stand in the way of the
hotel's expansion.[8]

The uneasy truce lasted only until one Sunday afternoon
in June 1903 when Waters visited Child at his hotel office at
Mammoth. The initial discussion was about some planned
meetings between Waters' Yellowstone Lake Boat Company
and all the other transportation companies in the park to see
if an agreement could be reached allowing the *Zillah* ride to
be a part of all tourist packages. F. Jay Haynes, the famed
photographer who was running his own stagecoach business
in Yellowstone, soon joined them in Child's office. With little
warning, though, Waters launched into a rant, accusing both
men of conspiring against his boat business. Both denied the
charge. When Child asked for specifics, Waters said that the
summer before Child had deliberately kept a high-ranking
military official named Corbin from seeing his steamboat and
taking a ride.

"Mr. Waters, this is entirely untrue because I was two or
three hundred miles away from the park when Adjutant General Corbin came here and did not see him at all," Child said
in recounting the episode in a letter.[9]

"That is a lie," Waters shot back. "You were in the park
and took Adjutant General Corbin through the park, and

purposefully kept him away from my boat and I know it."

"I wasn't here, I was in Helena," Child replied.

"You are a goddamn liar," barked Waters.

These were fighting words, certainly, but Child instead ordered a porter to escort Waters out of the hotel. As far as he was concerned, he and Waters were through. Later that week, Child wrote a letter to Pitcher detailing the incident, saying the Interior Department should never ask him to have "any business relations whatever with him in the future."

"Every person in the Park who has had any business relations with Mr. Waters since he has been in the Park knows that it is impossible to have any dealings with him that will result in a satisfactory manner," Child said.[9]

The next day after receiving that letter, Pitcher came into his office at Mammoth to sit down and write yet another letter imploring Interior Secretary Hitchcock to either kick Waters out of Yellowstone or at least allow competition that will "no doubt" force him into retirement.

"In one way or another he has been the source of almost every complaint that has come to your office," Pitcher told his boss. "Things have come to such a pass that no transportation company doing business in the park will now under any condition turn over a single passenger to Mr. Waters if they can possibly avoid it."[10]

He recognized the political and logistical difficulties of getting rid of Waters but urged Hitchcock to see it through. He signed off the letter: "The Department will never be free of complaints and annoyance until it has introduced this competition and rid itself of Mr. Waters."[10] But the Secretary did nothing, at least then.

After the summer season ended, Waters returned to Mammoth to meet with a man named William W. Wylie, a former school teacher and fellow entrepreneur in the park and, theoretically, a perfect ally for Waters. He, too, had come to Yellowstone in the early 1880s in the hopes of scratching out a living from the burgeoning tourist trade. His quarry was the slightly-less-rich clientele in the park. For those looking to spend less, Wylie set up a series of semi-permanent (and, later, permanent) camps , typically rows upon rows of canvas tent-cottages near dining halls, rest rooms, and baths. The Wylie camps became known as much for their unmistakably colored, striped canvas tents in the woods as the good-times, raucous customers they drew. Child and the railroad company did not care for Wylie's popular cut-rate camps and quickly recognized that it could eventually put some of their hotels out of business. In response, not only did they cut their hotel rates but also the Yellowstone Park Association banned Wylie from soliciting business on the railroad, in its hotels or at its other operations.[11]

Waters and Wylie had common foes in Child and the railroad but Waters' cantankerous nature would never allow an alliance to form. At the meeting in Mammoth that day, they were supposed to talk about Waters' payment for passengers on the Wylie tour who decided to take the steamboat. Waters tried to renege on an earlier agreement and the discussion went downhill fast. "Before we had talked five minutes he began his ugly flings and I got up and walked out and left him," Wylie said. "He threatened to sue us. I told him I was only too anxious to have it settled in court, and left him."[12]

Everywhere Waters turned during that summer of 1903, the stars seemed to be aligning against him: the railroad, the park managers, government overseers in D.C., his fellow businessmen and still more visitors.

"His trickery amounts to absolute swindling," one North

Dakota tourist complained after claiming Waters, in renting a fishing boat to her and her husband, had offered to
cover their fare if they didn't catch any fish and then smugly
reneged on the deal when they came back to shore empty-
handed. "Now I do not care in the least about the money he
swindled me out of, but I do not like to be 'done up' and then
laughed at." [13]

Waters decided it was time to launch a counter-offensive
before it was too late. He and his operatives quietly began col-
lecting sworn affidavits about the boat company, including
from several of his employees and a few stage coach drivers
who said Child, Haynes, hotel managers and others had, for
years, told Yellowstone travelers to stay away from the *Zillah*.

"Nearly every day someone would come down to look the
boat over and ask me if it was safe," J.T. Mellen, a stagecoach
driver, said in his testimony for Waters, "and some days there
would be three or four who would say they wanted to take the
steamer but had been told it was not safe and that their wives
and families would not dare to take the steamer." [14]

Since 1893, a number of spurious claims had been circu-
lated about the *Zillah*, one affidavit said, including that the
boat ride was treacherous, that its prices were too high, that
lightning was liable to strike it, that there was nothing to see
on the lake, that the steamer was "an old tub brought from
Lake Minnetonka, where it had sunk once and had been con-
demned" and that Waters was a "highway robber." [14]

By the time that a man named E.R. Palmer, in his second
year as a pilot of the *Zillah*, proffered his affidavit—in front
of Waters and his wife after swearing on a Bible—Waters'
bad behavior had gotten him temporarily barred from soliciting business to tourists ambling around Thumb or at the
Lake Hotel. Palmer said he was dismayed by the effort to take

down Waters' business. "I have never heard any one during that time say anything but praise of the steamer trip and during all that time I never heard any one say they thought Capt. Waters was 'obtrusive or impertinent,' on the contrary, I have heard many speak in the highest praise of his treatment and kindness to them and that they enjoyed hearing his stories very much," Palmer said.[14]

The affidavits, which of course contained only the highest praise, were compiled and bound in Wisconsin into a short paperback booklet, entitled *Explanation and Argument of The Yellowstone Lake Boat Co.* A copy found its way to park headquarters at Mammoth and likely was put into the hands of some of the most powerful people Waters could find.

Among the high-ranking political connections Waters exploited that year was New York Governor Benjamin B. Odell Jr., an influential force in the Republican Party. Waters had met Odell the previous summer during the governor's trip to Yellowstone. On state letterhead, Odell wrote a short note to President Roosevelt raising Waters' claims that "his company is in danger of being discriminated against." "He is an old New York man," Odell told the president, who himself was once a New York politician, "and I think the matter is of sufficient importance to have it looked into."[15]

Roosevelt, however, was already wise to Waters. Three days later, he wrote back to Governor Odell: "I am sorry to say that Waters has been in with a man named Fullerton in making a series of most vicious attacks upon the management of Yellowstone Park and upon the administration. Waters deserves no consideration at our hands. When I see you, I shall tell you in detail of the things he has done."[16]

Fullerton's deeds would become public soon enough. While his political friends mounted a campaign to save the boat business, Waters, ever the inveterate promoter, was spreading the word about his latest steamboat scheme to anyone who would listen. He again found willing ears again at the Wonderland newspaper in Gardiner. "Col. Waters was down from the Lake yesterday after the frame of his new steamboat," the paper reported in September 1903. "It will be completed long before the opening of the Park season next year."[17]

And the same Gardiner paper ran this item on October 10:

> We were favored on Thursday by a visit from Col. E. C. Waters, who is president and general manager of the boat company at Yellowstone lake. His family will soon leave for Fond du Lac, Wis., where they will remain until early summer, while he will go to his large cattle and sheep ranch near Billings, and look after his interests there. Mr. Waters says his company is building and has nearly completed a new steamboat for the lake at a cost of not less than $60,000. It will carry 300 passengers and will take the place of the 'Zillah' now in use and which will be put in use on the Cody line. The lake is one of the prettiest bodies of water on earth, and the new boat will be able to handle the constantly increasing business.[18]

The following month, a newspaper in Minneapolis announced that the Zillah was being dismantled "and will be replaced by a new steamer, modeled after those that ply the Long Island sound between New York and New London."[19]

As 1903 drew toward a close, Wylie wrote to Pitcher in the superintendent's office about Waters' big plans for a new steamboat on the lake. "Yes, I notice often notices of the grand new steamer," Wylie sniffed. "I really do not believe he means to build a new steamer. I think it is a big bluff."[20]

It was no bluff. But before Waters put his plan into action, he decided to see if he could clear a better path to success by stirring the political pot in the hopes of prying some of his enemies, especially the bristly superintendent, John Pitcher, out of their seats of power.

10 UNDER FIRE

In the winter of 1903, a letter to the editor appeared in the *Washington Post* from a man named James Fullerton, a farmer, taxidermist, and hunter from Red Lodge, Montana, a small mining town in the Beartooth Mountains, just outside Yellowstone. The subject was trouble in Yellowstone. Fullerton, self-righteous and slightly unhinged, had been traveling in Yellowstone and was astonished to find that, despite strict rules forbidding it, "unlimited quantities" of alcohol were being served at every hotel in the park. Fullerton photographed the drinkers and barrooms and began raising a ruckus[1].

The *New York Times* picked up Fullerton's complaints when he stopped in Omaha, Nebraska, on his way to see Congress in Washington, D.C. "We have been trying to get an investigation into the rotten condition of affairs in the Yellowstone Park," Fullerton wrote to Congress, saying those conditions included "venality and corruption." "I stand prepared to furnish indisputable proof that the President, the Assistant Secretary of the Interior, and Major Pitcher, Superintendent of the park, have been in collusion for a year to allow H.W. Childs [sic] to run a lot of illegal saloons in Yellow Stone Park," Fullerton said.[2]

Fullerton called himself president of the "Sportsman's Game Protective Association," had written for sporting journals, and knew many of the same men that often accompanied President Roosevelt on his outdoor adventures.[3]

Fullerton also wrote a lacerating letter to a Republican congressman from Iowa named John F. Lacey, one of Yellowstone's earliest defenders and author of the Lacey Act that helped combat poaching. In his letter, Fullerton accused Lacey and other Republicans of being too soft on Roosevelt (an "arrant coward") and Pitcher ("the notorious blackguard"), and ignoring "disgusting conduct" in Yellowstone. Pitcher, he wrote, "told a lot of drunken, vulgar brutes of his own class to go ahead and insult a number of ladies and foreigners by singing OBSCENE!!! and PROFANE songs in the halls of the Canyon hotel and permitted a reign of terror all night." "You may think that you and the other cowards that are afraid to have that dirty gang of scoundrels in the interior department exposed before election will get off without it being known, but you are sadly off your base," Fullerton wrote.[4]

Pitcher was on a trip to California that winter. When he returned to Mammoth, he found a letter addressed to him from Congressman Lacey and a copy of Fullerton's letter. The superintendent quickly familiarized himself with Fullerton. His "Sportsman's Game Protective Association" in Red Lodge was, in fact, a group of just one man. And, during one trip to Yellowstone, Fullerton tried to get the son of a prominent senator to secure him a job as the park's game warden, Pitcher learned. The gambit failed. Pitcher wrote back to Lacey, saying Fullerton was a "contemptible whelp" and "an unmitigated fraud to say the least."[4]

He then added: "I have good evidence that he has been in the past, and is probably now, employed by Mr. E. C. Waters, the president of the Yellowstone Lake Boat Company, for the purpose of stirring up all the trouble he possibly can for both myself and every one else connected with the administration of affairs in the park." Indeed, he said there was "undoubted truth" that Waters had instigated Fullerton's letter to the *Washington Post* and paid for his trip to Washington, D.C. Again Waters demonstrated a disturbing willingness to do anything to further his business that exceeded simple entrepreneurial zealousness, Pitcher said. "His rambling communications referring to many subjects, are a nuisance to everyone, and confirm the suggestion made some time since that he is mentally disordered," Pitcher said.[4]

As for Fullerton, he eventually got a personal audience with Roosevelt but then squandered it by calling Pitcher, the president's good friend, a "grafter" for ignoring alcohol in Yellowstone. Fullerton later claimed Roosevelt was scared to address drinking in the park for fear of upsetting the Northern Pacific Railway. He also offered a wild story that, because of his complaints about Yellowstone and Pitcher, Roosevelt had him arrested and committed to an insane asylum in Montana for two weeks where he was "thrown into a den of syphilitic idiots." This allegation did Fullerton no good whatsoever and in fact made him look as crazy as Waters was beginning to look to many observers.[5]

The highly public attempt by Waters and Fullerton to drive out Pitcher ultimately did little more than anger Pitcher and Roosevelt. No one else took it seriously.

In the summer of 1904, the safety of steamboats became horrific front page news. On June 14, the enormous *General Slocum* caught fire and sank on New York's East River while taking members of a Lutheran church to a picnic. More than 1,000 people drowned or died in the fire. Investigators said many of the lifejackets were so old they crumbled in the hands of the desperate and some of the boat's life rafts were stuck in place and thus unusable when the moment came. As news of the Slocum spread, Pitcher sent a telegram to Waters, asking whether "in light of the terrible disasters" the *Zillah* had been properly inspected and equipped with life-saving apparatus. Waters, perhaps rightfully defensive, shot back the next day that his boat was inspected every year and had all the proper equipment. The disaster apparently did not dampen tourists' enthusiasm for the *Zillah*—more than 3,800 people rode it that summer.[6]

Tensions, though, continued to rise between Waters, the park superintendent, and the Yellowstone Park Association, and came to a head later in the summer. The trouble started in July 1904 with a complaint from Harry Child that Waters had hired away a porter at the Lake Hotel for more money, breaking a long standing gentleman's agreement that those doing business in the park would not poach each other's employees. Waters immediately composed a four-page telegram after hearing the complaint from Pitcher, vehemently denying he had hired anyone from the hotel (although he admitted he had hired at least one man who had been fired). Waters then turned the tables on Child, saying the man in charge of the crew that collected hay for the hotel had hired away some of his men the previous year and that he had also secretly pulled a coupling pin out of one of Waters' wagons, putting it out of commission until a replacement part arrived from Livingston, some one hundred miles away from Lake.[7]

Around that same time, Waters also irritated photographer F. Jay Haynes, who had a long and fairly unblemished record as a businessman in Yellowstone. At one point, Waters implicated Haynes in a "dynamite incident," a cryptic reference that, although not fully explained in Waters' letter, drew Haynes' wrath. "When a man has the hallucination that everyone in the park is trying to rob him…it is but natural to expect that he will publish vile pamphlets and attempt in every possible way to blackguard them," Haynes said. "His assertion pertaining to the dynamite incident is an unmitigated falsehood emanating from his diseased imagination." That letter, with its implications of mental instability, would soon come back to haunt Waters. [8]

The next day, Pitcher sent Haynes' comments to the Secretary of the Interior, urging him to note Haynes' comments "concerning the sanity of Mr. Waters." "His curious charges and his peculiar actions during the past three years lead me to believe that there must be considerable truth in the suggestion of Mr. Haynes that he is crazy, and if this is the case he is certainly unfit to carry on the boat business on the lake in the Park," Pitcher wrote. [8]

Child, who was constantly growing more powerful in Yellowstone, also began putting the squeeze on Waters the following month, first banning him and all of his employees from the lunch station at Thumb (where Waters would often recruit passengers for the *Zillah*) and then from all the hotels operated by the Yellowstone Park Association, including Lake Hotel, which Waters had haunted for years, especially since his summer home was just a few steps away. Child said it was because Waters and his workers were "making themselves obnoxious to our guests by soliciting business under false statements and misrepresentations." [9]

Waters found out on a Sunday afternoon in mid-August that he was banned from a business in his own area. When he arrived at Thumb, the lunch station manager, George Spencer, told him that he could no longer eat there, spend money there, or even be on the premises. If necessary, Spencer told Waters, he had been authorized to remove him by force. Waters was flabbergasted. The next day one of Waters' employees was kicked out of the Lake Hotel. The boat captain quickly filed a complaint to the superintendent about "this great injustice." "We are American citizens, have never made any disturbance in any house in the Park or in any way broken any of the rules," Waters protested.[10]

Stung and humiliated, Waters pushed ahead. He returned to Thumb a few days later, apparently with grudging permission from Pitcher, and put up a single tent along the wooden walkway to the steamboat dock to serve as his office. It was a small and pathetic gesture but also a signal that he had no intention of relenting.[11]

Soon Waters wrote another long and rambling letter to top officials at the Department of the Interior claiming, among other things, that Yellowstone Park Association had hired away his "Chinaman" cook and that Pitcher had a financial interest in Child's transportation company that was actively discouraging visitors from boarding the *Zillah*.[12] Pitcher seethed, calling Waters an "unmitigated liar" and reiterated that allowing a competing steamboat on Yellowstone Lake would be the simplest way to get rid of Waters and his company, "the most objectionable features we have in the Park today."[13]

As the tumultuous 1904 summer tourist season ended in Yellowstone, Waters took his family to Gardiner and put them on the train to spend the winter and spring at the family home in Fond du Lac. No doubt still wounded, Waters settled onto his ranch outside Billings.

That December, newspapers published a notice that Waters had completed work on his new steamer at Yellowstone

Lake, at the cost of three years and several thousand dollars. It would be running on the lake the following summer, came the claim. "The steamer has accommodations for 700 passengers and will be the finest craft afloat between the Great Lakes and Puget Sound," said the *Minneapolis Journal.*[14]

If there were any high spirits left in Waters that winter in Montana, they must have danced a little in anticipation over the new boat. Any jubilation, however, was short-lived.

11 UNMOORED AND ADRIFT

Young Anna Waters spent most of the summers of her life in Yellowstone, exploring its extraordinary hot springs, marveling at its wildlife (sometimes straying dangerously close to bears), and rubbing elbows with the rich travelers who stayed at the Lake Hotel and rode the *Zillah*. She also witnessed her father's endless battles with the park's powers-that-be and no doubt heard and endured his evening rants about every possible slight and conspiracy against him.

At home in Fond du Lac, Anna was a studious girl who, like her mother, loved classic literature, and was thought of as a "deep thinker" who was popular in social circles. The winter was a difficult one. Anna's aunt (her mother's sister) Anna D. Amory had died. As one of seven beneficiaries in the will, young Anna was the recipient of a small fortune. But she suffered from depression and in the final weeks of 1904, eighteen-year-old Anna was in a "disconsolate state of mind." Her friends and family tried time and again to cheer her up but she remained lonely and melancholy. Some of that was certainly typical teenage angst—she complained after a party that she "felt stupid" the whole time she was there—but her dark streak ran deeper than most knew. [1]

On January 6, 1905, Anna ate lunch with her family at the Waters home on Fourth Street and then went to a nearby drug store, where she bought a bottle of chloroform. Back at the house, she chatted with some boys playing in the billiards room and, minutes later, shut herself in the bathroom and poisoned herself with a combination of chloroform and carbolic acid (though the acid was said to be diluted and used for brushing teeth). There was a noise from the bathroom, "Oh, oh!" Family members rushed in and found Anna disappearing into unconsciousness. Three doctors spent forty-five minutes desperately trying to revive her but she never returned. By 3 P.M., she was dead.

"Members of the Waters family firmly believe that the melancholia with which she was affected was undoubtedly the cause of her premeditating suicide," said one newspaper story that ran with the headline "Was Tired of Living."[1]

Word of Anna's death reached E. C. Waters in Red Lodge, Montana, the next day. Stricken with grief he immediately boarded a train for a terrible, thousand-mile trip back to Wisconsin. A week after Anna's funeral at the family home, Waters wrote a pained and blistering letter:

> To the many that have kindly written and wired their condolences in this hour of our great bereavement from nearly every state in the Union and to those of our friends who have expressed a wish to know what prompted this desperate action on the part of our beloved daughter, I wish to say:

That we believe it was fear of financial ruin, despondency and humiliation over our business troubles, caused by the indignities, falsehoods and vituperation heaped upon our business in the Yellowstone National Park by H.W. Child, President of the Hotel and Transportation Co., F. Jay Haynes, President of the Monida and Yellowstone Stage Co., Major John Pitcher, Superintendent of the Yellowstone Park, the Northern Pacific Railroad Co., and others.

To those who have never been in the Park I will explain by saying: That I am President of the Yellowstone Lake Boat Co., that myself and family own the controlling interest in said company, which has a lease from the United States Government to conduct a steamboat business on Yellowstone Lake.

Now the Northern Pacific Railroad Company own and control a majority of the stock in the Hotel and Transportation Company and wish to control everything in the Park including The Boat Company, (or get a steamboat of their own on Yellowstone Lake) which if allowed means financial ruin to us.

For the past few years they have through their agents and employees used every means possible to keep people off the steamer and in every way have discredited our business by misrepresentations and slander, hoping in the end to get control of our company. Many, many times has my beloved daughter begged me "to give up everything in the Park rather than suffer these indignities and slander." She told her girl friend, when I was in Washington D.C., last winter this: "I think it is money and time wasted for Papa to go to Washington to try to do anything because I know the N.P.R.R.

Co. has lots of money and as bribery and corruption is the order of things with Railway and Trust Companies right now, I feel sure there is no chance for Papa and The Boat Company to get their just dues."

A few days before her death she said to the same girl friend that she believed "The N.P.R.R. Co. and their assistants would ruin us." She also stated to her mother a few days before she died that "I know we will not use any of the money that aunt left me because I know we will be financially ruined by these people in our Park business and I want to keep that money to care for Mamma and all of us with."

A few days before she died she said to her friend: "I am so worried about my father and the Park business," and saying "my Papa is getting old, he works too hard looking after the business there and with all these indignities and slander heaped upon him I fear he will not stand the strain."

These are the unquestionable proofs of the cause of this dutiful, loving and beloved daughter's death. She had no troubles of her own. She died because she was burdened with these business troubles. She had a very sensitive organization and could not live longer under this fear of financial disaster to her family and stand the thought of the indignities and slander heaped upon us.

Thanking you for all the kind words of sympathy and condolence as well as assistance offered from many, I remain a heart-broken man and father.

Yours most sincerely, E. C. Waters.[2]

It was an astonishing outpouring, perhaps most because he seems to have reflexively wielded this awful tragedy as ammunition against his enemies. Indeed it is possible that Waters' troubles in Yellowstone may have been a central cause in her death—history has left unrecorded conversations between father and daughter—but Waters' letter is the only indication that was the case and it seems suspicious that an eighteen-year-old girl could be so swept up in her father's business affairs. This particular desperation would ring more true if she had been told that her father's very physical existence was at stake, and perhaps that happened. On its face, however, it seems most likely that Anna Waters took her life for reasons beyond her father's difficulties in the national park and that he made up the entire story. Waters had likely become so consumed by park affairs that he struggled to view any event as unrelated to that prism, whether he knew it or not. And the grief of losing a child and plunging into utter turmoil manifests itself in all manner of extreme and sometimes strange reactions. Waters certainly would not be the last to misdirect such agony.

It is unclear who exactly got copies of the letter but it is likely that Waters distributed it far and wide. One copy found its way to Yellowstone's headquarters at Mammoth, but Waters never mentioned Anna's death again in his correspondence with those at the park.

He remained in Fond du Lac for a time but returned to Yellowstone that spring to oversee the construction of his new ship—and found that, while he was agonizing over his family's loss, little had changed in the park. By July, he was again filing complaints with the superintendent, this time that a porter at the Upper Geyser Hotel was bad-mouthing the *Zillah*, telling tourists that it was likely to end up at the bottom of the lake. The porter was also apparently selling fishing tackle, nosing his way into Waters' fishing business on the lake. "I know from reliable sources that this porter is acting with Mr. Child's knowledge, and I believe under his instruction," Waters said.[3]

Pitcher relayed the complaint to an exasperated Child at the company's office in Mammoth. "Can there be no relief granted the two companies I am operating…from Mr. Waters' repeated insulting attacks?" Child responded.[3]

What *was* different that summer of 1905 is that the tourism business in Yellowstone was exploding. More people visited the park that summer—a number exceeding 26,000—than any other year. The previous year had been Yellowstone's best that far, yet twice as many people came to the park in 1905. A fascination with the West hung in the air that summer, largely because it was the centennial of the Lewis and Clark expedition. Portland, Oregon, held a massive celebration—something akin to a "world's fair"—attended by more than a million people. Many of them arrived by train as the Northern Pacific Railway, which never missed a chance to wring more money out of the traveling public, funneled westbound travelers to Yellowstone on their way to Oregon. "We expect next season will be the biggest year we have had since the opening of Yellowstone Park," W.W. Wylie predicted in January.[4]

Wylie was right. Hotels in the park were packed that summer, as were the stagecoaches, camps and even the *Zillah*. Yellowstone had never been more popular or prosperous. It seemed the perfect time to launch the *E. C. Waters*.

It is unclear exactly when the first pieces of the ship that would eventually become the *E. C. Waters* arrived in the park, but it was probably 1903 or 1904. Just getting the parts to the shores of Yellowstone Lake where the ship was to be assembled was a Herculean task. Little had changed since the

Zillah was hauled in more than a decade before. Yellowstone remained an isolated and mostly primitive destination, and anything that was brought into the park arrived at a sluggish and deliberate pace at the whims of weather, distance, and the horse teams that labored up high mountain passes and along shabby roads. Worse still, each piece had to be small enough to be pulled in a single wagon, and if it was not, it had to be cut into smaller pieces to fit.

Waters' new ship required a cylindrical Scotch boiler— a twelve-foot-long steel behemoth fitted with furnaces that burned wood to convert water to steam—that were built in Ferrysburg, Michigan, and shipped by rail to Gardiner. Its design gave a Scotch boiler a shorter time to "get up steam," and such boilers were relatively compact (though heavy). From Gardiner, teamsters hauled the boiler in horse-drawn wagons to an impromptu shipyard on the lake shore.[5] Other parts included the four-bladed, cast-iron propeller six feet in diameter, a network of piping and valves, and a hulking engine system from Montague, Michigan. The Douglas-fir that formed the hull and much of the boat's superstructure was hauled in from Oregon. Oak was used for the keel and frame.[6]

And then there were the hundreds of other smaller parts: valves, bolts, fittings, railings, brass keyhole plates for the doors, inch-thick glass for the passenger windows. How many nights had Waters stayed up worrying about these shipments and their safe passage over Yellowstone's bone-rattling roads?

Building the steamship was a massive undertaking. Nothing like it had ever been built in such a high-elevation, isolated environment. The weather at Yellowstone Lake, even in the summer, was fickle and often fierce—sunny and warm one moment, and raining or even snowing the next. Little is known about the men who actually built the *E. C. Waters* but they were apparently experienced, assembling a highly competent vessel with few mistakes during what was likely a rushed job during the short construction season in the Wyoming mountains. There were some anomalies, however, including that the framing style of the hull in the bow and the stern was different from that of midships, raising the possibility that there were two different men in charge of the ship's construction or that parts of it were salvaged from another ship.[7]

As the summer months wore on, Waters no doubt obsessed over the boat's progress. The make-shift shipyard, complete with a marine railway to haul it in and out of the lake, was within easy sight of the docks at Lake and it is not difficult to imagine Waters, puffed with pride in the perch of the pilot house in the *Zillah*, daydreaming about finally launching his masterpiece vessel. It was, of course, more than a ship. It was a testament and a protest and a declaration of stubborn survival. He had withstood attacks and grief, and triumphed. Even when he could have and probably *should have* left Yellowstone, he stayed and pressed on alone. What did he believe in? Himself? Or perhaps the belief that, given enough time, his rivals in Yellowstone would be exposed and brought low, clearing the way in his head for his own ascension into a long-denied world of prosperity and power. That may have been his most potent hallucination. Or maybe he had no higher belief system at all beyond the sheer animal instinct to survive in a hostile world for as long as possible.

Whatever the case, the ship was finally becoming real for all to see, including visitors who were being treated to the exotic sights and sounds of this stately ship, 125 feet from bow to stern, under construction on the shores of Yellowstone Lake.

Like the *Zillah*, the *E. C. Waters* showcased an enclosed lower deck for those looking to escape the lake's brisk breezes and a sprawling, covered promenade-deck above so that travelers could walk freely to take in the sights from the railing in every direction, including the beloved Teton Range to the south, and the teeth-shaped Absaroka Range to the east. Once most of the three-story boat was built, it was hauled to Stevenson Island for "fitting out," mostly painting and upholstery and other work that would give the ship its final, regal touches. Ever wary of potential trouble from his enemies, Waters ordered a cabin built on the edge of the island's beach so that one of his men could keep watch over his precious project.[8]

The ship remained unfinished as the 1905 tourist season drew to a close but Waters, anxious to finally show off what he had done, decided to christen it anyway. He planned it for September 16, a Saturday, a day he knew would be sure to draw the biggest crowds. That morning, however, a stiff gale persisted on the lake, kicking up high waves and forcing Waters to call off his unveiling. Clearly, spectators were undeterred: when the rescheduled event took place Monday morning, some three hundred people showed up from around Yellowstone. The emcee was F.D. Geiger of the *Wonderland* newspaper in Gardiner. The influential editor was one of the few people Waters had wisely managed not to alienate in his nearly two decades at Yellowstone. The paper provided gushing coverage of the ceremony in a lengthy and splashy, front-page story a few days later that called Waters a "brave and generous pioneer of the park" and the ship "the greatest boat the northwest ever had."[9]

The ceremony itself lasted less than an hour. Much of it was filled by a speech read by Geiger (but written by a former mayor of Livingston) lavishly recounting Waters' years in

Yellowstone, including his arrival so many years earlier when his children were young and "the most enlightened" observers scoffed at his foolish plans to bring the *Zillah* into Yellowstone. "With the small tourist travel of those days, perhaps no other man in America would have undertaken the placing of a steam boat on Lake Yellowstone. Aside from the apparent impossibility of the undertaking, the financial side of the enterprise looked very shady," Geiger told the crowd.

"For sixteen years the *Zillah* freighted with human souls has made her trips to and from the thumb of the lake to the Lake Hotel, she has carried the rich and the poor, the old and the young, the great people, and the Smiths and never has one of her passengers needed a life preserver or a bathing suit....Her name and fame are coextensive with that of the great lake, the waters of which have been held in her sole dominion since navigation began," Geiger gushed.

"But Col. Waters is an expansionist," he went on.

> He sees clearly that the little boat of which he speaks as fondly as though it were a daughter can no longer satisfy the demands of the sightseeing public, and hence this delightful occasion. We are here to launch the splendid new steamer upon the lake. Not only so, but we are here to honor the man who had risked his fortune and who has spent the best years of his life in bettering the conditions of public travel through the greatest collection of nature wonders now upon earth.

Mr. Geiger continued: "At no time have the relations between those of the outside world and those in control of all departments governing and managing the entire park been so cordial and so happy."

Now, Geiger said, "the proud '*Zillah*' with her banners gently waving to and fro in the breezes of time, has made her journey to and from the thumb to the wrist, ever carrying her precious burden of human freight who were on pleasure bent, sightseeing as it were, in the greatest park in the entire world."

Under brighter circumstances, it is likely that Waters would have chosen his youngest daughter, Anna, to christen his prized new steamship. She had been young and pretty and the picture of a life at the brink of promise and fortune. Instead, Waters turned to his unmarried, twenty-one-year-old daughter Edna. She cut a grim figure on the dock, wearing a dark suit, a black hat, long black gloves, and a conspicuous black band on one arm, and carrying a dozen American Beauty roses shipped in from Helena. At the proper moment, she smashed a large bottle of champagne onto the bow, declared it the *E. C. Waters*, and watched as it slipped into the lake.

Certainly the ceremony was more than bittersweet for Waters. The loss of his youngest daughter, two decades of war with Yellowstone's military leaders and his own competitors, and the relentless prospect of ruin and disgrace had taken a toll—he must have been exhausted. Simultaneously, the boat loomed as a new, invigorating force in his life promising salvation, stability, and honor. No more rickety *Zillah*, no more petty complaints, and finally a legitimate enterprise that would secure his finances and his place in Yellowstone's history.

A fawning story in the *Wonderland* later that week was infused with Waters' grandiosity. The *E. C. Waters*, declared editor Geiger, was the "Pride of Yellowstone Lake" and the man who brought it to the park "will pass into history as one of the west's great promoters." "The new boat slipped from its moorings into the deep lake with great ease and comfort and looked perfectly at home upon the deep blue waters of the highest lake in the whole world," the newspaper said.[9]

The christening, however, was not a real beginning, but the beginning of the end. Although a few people did ride on the *E. C. Waters* that day, when the season closed, no one had paid and there had been no profit. And the powers that controlled Yellowstone wanted to make sure it stayed that way.

12 A GATHERING STORM

When the summer tourist season arrived in Yellowstone in June 1906, Waters must have brimmed with new hope. Crews on Stevenson Island were putting the finishing touches on the *E. C. Waters*, including paint and some last-minute upholstery. Waters sent a confident letter to Superintendent Pitcher that the huge ship would be ready for hundreds of paying customers on July 1. Pitcher and Interior Secretary Ethan Hitchcock wanted nothing of the sort. While final preparations were continuing with the *E. C. Waters*, Hitchcock sent a stern letter to the Yellowstone superintendent ordering that the *Zillah* be inspected to show it was "seaworthy" and that the inspector state what the maximum number of passengers would be. He also wanted all of Waters' rowboats inspected "by a competent person." [1]

Waters, sensing trouble, seethed. He shot back a long, defensive response to Pitcher, saying the *Zillah* had, every year, undergone a yearly "painstaking inspection" by a federal safety official. "He has crawled into the boiler each year and tested every stay bolt in her, has inspected every pump, valve, lifeboat, life preserver, life raft, safety valve; in fact every flange and every part of the machinery and equipment in the most careful and minute way," Waters protested. Every suggested improvement had been made, every U.S. marine law followed, nary a passenger had been hurt or lost over sixteen years and not a single passenger had been allowed to ride the *Zillah* beyond its limit of 120 per trip, he fumed. "It would seem to us that this record should be some guarantee to the Hon. Secretary of the Interior that the management of this company's business has been conducted in a proper way, and should be entitled to some little confidence," Waters added. [1]

He instinctively turned the focus onto his enemies. Rather than attack the Yellowstone Boat Company, Waters said the park and the traveling public would be better served if inspectors cracked down on the illegal sale of liquor in the hotels and the charges of up to $6 for a bath "of which there is bitter complaint made," Waters said. He went on to accuse Child's transportation company of crowding eleven people onto coaches built for seven and the Monida company of forcing guests at Old Faithful Inn to wake up at 5 or 5:30 each morning to catch its coach to Thumb. Finally he complained that Pitcher and his staff had, time and again, failed to follow through on their promise to print up a pamphlet for travelers saying the *Zillah* is "staunch and safe." These were small grievances, all, but Waters felt like he had been at the receiving end of complaints for longer than he could stand it. [1]

The summer of 1906 was not a repeat of 1905's robust business for Yellowstone, but more than 5,000 people rode the *Zillah* that summer, not bad for a boat that some thought was on its last legs. The *E. C. Waters*, however, remained moored and unused because it still did not have final approval from the park. Waters' business, though, still drew more complaints than any other in the park. A factory owner from Indiana said the small fishing boat he and his companions rented from Waters' company leaked so badly they had to go to shore twice to empty it out and spent the rest of the time with their feet in three inches of water sloshing around the boat's bottom. He also complained that his party was given an unwieldy and cumbersome boat when they declined to pay the extra fifty cents per hour for one of Waters' employees to row the boat for them. That complaint was guaranteed to receive attention because it suggested vengeance. "It looks as if the boat business in Yellowstone was a holdup," the man said.[2]

Something else secretive was going on that summer on the shores of Yellowstone Lake. Waters' daughter, Edna—in typical park fashion—had fallen in love with a clerk at Lake Hotel. Her romance with A.F. Molina unfolded quickly and, by the end of the summer, Molina asked E. C. Waters if he could marry his daughter. Waters refused because, according to one account, Molina was "unknown to the family." Molina left Yellowstone for Seattle as the tourist season wound down in mid-September. Two weeks later, Edna told her parents she was going back East to visit friends. From Livingston, she took the train one stop to the east, got off and hopped on the first westbound train straight to Seattle. Two days later, the couple married. The wedding made the papers, calling E. C. Waters "the millionaire lumberman of Fond du Lac, Wis." and pointedly noted that the nuptials had not been blessed by the father of the bride. "Mr. and Mrs. D'Molina will start East at once and brave his wrath," said report said.[3]

Waters, however, had his mind on his business. Around

the same time in Yellowstone, the *E. C. Waters* passed its final inspection and even made a trial run. Delayed again, the boat would nevertheless be ready for business at the opening of the 1907 season, Waters told the Interior Department. "This boat is a very fine one and is first class in every particular," said Waters, who clearly knew of the department's opposition to his ship. "She will have a fine electric plant, search light and show lights. She carries two more lifeboats than the law requires and has all modern life saving appliances. It is heated by steam."[4]

The year ended with a sad and strange episode involving a man named Dave Edwards, a "winter keeper" hired by Waters to keep an eye on the *E. C. Waters* at Stevenson Island. It was a lonely mission—he was equipped with a tiny, stove-heated cabin on the knoll of the island and nothing but empty hours to fill. One day in the fall, as he was rowing out to the island, he suffered a heart attack. His body was discovered in the drifting row boat and brought to Lake by soldiers. The next day, they telephoned headquarters in Mammoth and dictated a list of Edwards' effects: a gold watch and chain, a pair of gold-rimmed spectacles, a pocket knife, a pipe, keys, $3.40 in cash, a trunk (taken from the island) and a letter with undisclosed contents "from Miss Hattie Murphy" of Livingston, Montana.[5]

Edwards was buried somewhere between Waters' house at Lake and the lake's outlet. Waters, however planned to dig up his body and send it to back to Alta, Iowa, where Edwards was from.[6] Apparently that never happened. The following summer, a human skull—with its left ear and a few teeth still attached—washed up on the south shore of Stevenson Island, and it was believed to be that one of one of two men who drowned in the lake the previous summer. The skull was placed in a box and buried "inside the grave of Dave Edwards."[7] Decades later, the gravesite was paved over for a gas station.[8]

Edwards could be replaced. The fate of his business, Waters learned soon, was much more tenuous. His ten-year contract to operate steamboats on the lake expired in January 1907. Although he had been told a year earlier that his contract would be renewed, the Department of the Interior was now casting doubts on that plan. His huge investment into the *E. C. Waters*—still moored on the island in the middle of the lake—was threatened.

In October 1906, Pitcher filed his annual report to the Interior Department as usual, but this time noting that Waters and his business were the worst they had ever been in the past eighteen years. "It is about time to end it," Pitcher said, reiterating the need to allow competing businesses to run passenger boats on the lake and adding that Wylie's business might be interested along with the Monida and Yellowstone Stage Company. Waters had heard that the government was again keen to have a competing steamboat on the lake and that the primary interest came from the railroad-backed companies that ran Yellowstone's hotels and transportation. His information came from a secret source, a friend in Washington, D.C., who "has means of knowing what is going on in the Interior Department." The friend, according to Waters, said the government was intent on completing a monopoly for the tourist business in Yellowstone for the hotel and transportation companies by denying Waters' boat lease and handing it over to his competitors. "They say it is the best thing in the Park and that the whole thing ought to be in the hands of one company as it would be of less trouble to the Department," Waters quoted his friend as saying. The boat lease on

Yellowstone Lake was seen as "essential to the completion of their intended and much desired absolute dominion over the entire park."[9]

Waters did not dare disclose the name of his friend but put every ounce of confidence in his information. Clearly some of it was off-base; the claim that the boat business was the "best thing in the park" was dubious given Waters' marginal profits and history of trouble.[9]

Nonetheless, the Yellowstone Lake Boat Company was staring into the face of failure. If the contract was not renewed, the boat business would be ruined and, most likely, so would Waters. He took some comfort in knowing that Interior Secretary Ethan A. Hitchcock was leaving office that winter to be replaced by James Rudolph Garfield, son of former President James A. Garfield. Hitchcock, the longest-serving Interior secretary until that point, clearly had no love for Waters; the new secretary might provide an opportunity for a clean slate. Still, Waters knew his problems were bigger than he could handle; if he was going to defeat a gathering of his enemies working in concert against him he would need more firepower.

As he had done time and again, he found a powerful, well-connected political figure to do his bidding. This time it was William Bourke Cockran, an Irish-American lawyer and congressman from New York known for his powerful oratory skills. Waters met Cockran in the summer of 1906 at the lunch station at Thumb while Cockran was touring Yellowstone with his new (and third) wife Annie. They spent days on the exhausting stagecoach and Cockran was happy to bump into Waters and hear about the boat ride across the lake, anything to get a break from the dirt and tedium of Yellowstone's primitive dust-choked roads. "This sail proved to be the best feature of the entire trip," Cockran said. [10]

Aboard the *Zillah*, Cockran told Waters that he was surprised that the boat ride had never been mentioned by any of the hotels or the stagecoach drivers. Waters seized the opening, explaining that he believed the company controlling hotels and transportation wanted to drive him out of the park and take over his exclusive lease to run boats on the lake. Cockran was "deeply moved" by Waters' story and, once he got to the Lake Hotel, decided to ask around for more. Although the government officials and those who ran the stagecoaches complained about Waters, others at Lake "openly sympathized with Captain Waters, and expressed the belief that he was the object of a plot by powerful influence who coveted his business." The old boat captain, Cockran decided, was in a "struggle for justice against overwhelming odds." [10]

The day after his ride on the *Zillah*, Cockran sought out the stagecoach driver he had ridden with earlier—"a most respectable, thoughtful and intelligent man"—and asked why the driver had never mentioned Waters' boat ride. "He answered after some hesitation, that the boat service being independent of the stage and hotel companies, he was instructed not to mention it in conversation," Cockran said. [10]

Before he left Yellowstone, Cockran wrote Waters a letter offering help in his predicament. Waters did not write back immediately but took Cochran's letter back home to Fond du Lac that winter. When news came that his contract might not be renewed, Waters penned Cockran a long, detailed letter with the history of his steamboat business and a plea to use his political connections to save his business and, indeed, his life's earnings. Any attempt to kill his lease and give the boat business to his competitors must be crushed, Waters pleaded, lest Yellowstone be further delivered into the hands of a powerful few. "It turns everything in the Park to these companies and makes a monopoly of the national pleasure ground," he wrote. "I earnestly urge you to assist me, an old veteran of '61 to '65, in the effort to secure from a government he fought [for] to save his just dues and not allow a lot of grafters to despoil and leave me penniless in old age."[11]

Back in Washington, D.C., Garfield, the new Interior secretary, arrived and quickly dashed Waters' hopes that he would be a sympathetic ear. Clearly he had been briefed on Waters and his history in the park and seemed determined to drive him out, or at least to scare him a bit. A week after taking office, Garfield sent a list of demands to Waters, asking for details about the worth of his company, who his stockholders were, how many people had ridden the *Zillah* recently, and what arrangements he had for cooperating with the Northern Pacific Railway Company as well as the Yellowstone Park Association, Yellowstone Park Transportation Company, and others operating in the park. The terse letter showed no indication about whether Waters' boat business would continue in Yellowstone.[12]

Three weeks later, the Interior Department notified Waters' attorneys in New York that his lease would be extended, but only for one year, not the ten years he had hoped for. The boat lease would expire in January 1908—and then the lake tourism business would finally be opened up to competition. Waters found the letter from Interior waiting for him when he returned to Fond du Lac from Montana in late April 1907. It made him believe that Yellowstone was slipping out of his hands along with the business that had consumed so much of his life, his money, his wife's money, and surely some of his mental health. But on close reading, Waters noticed the new proposed lease lacked an important provision from his earlier contracts: an option for the government to either buy him out or renew his lease for another ten years. When Interior Secretary John Noble kicked George Wakefield out of Yellowstone in 1890, he compelled the incoming transportation company (with Silas Huntley at the helm) to write Wakefield a check for his troubles. Waters, who had been part of the Wakefield end, now wanted the same treatment.

The government had no interest in buying Waters out and the omission of that clause from the contract was no accident. Waters knew that any chance of getting out of Yellowstone with any cash at all was disappearing fast. His life's savings were tied up in the boat business, as was all the money that his wife received in her father's will. He was now fifty-eight, and desperate under the weight of possible ruin.

He went to New York but quickly fell ill and had to be hospitalized, likely with the first severe symptoms of the tuberculosis that would wrack his body a few years later. Bedridden, he lost precious weeks as the fate of his business unfolded without him. Finally, near the end of May 1907, he penned another fretful letter to Bourke Cockran, this time pleading for him to take the case to his friend in the White House, Theodore Roosevelt. Cockran and Roosevelt had known each other for years. If Roosevelt and Interior Secretary Garfield would simply re-insert the provision of the old contract or extend the lease for another ten to twenty years, Waters said, he would have a shot at survival. If nothing else it would give him time to sell his company's property to Child's company, which he knew had deep financial ties to the Northern Pacific Railway. [13]

It must have stung Waters to write those words. The railroad company and all the pet businesses it controlled in Yellowstone had been Waters' sworn enemies for years, and now he was asking the government—his other longstanding adversary—to allow him to sell out to the railroad, to allow the entire enterprise that he had built from nothing to be swallowed by the very beast he had fought for so long.

The alternative was even uglier. When the lease ran out in a year— along with his legal right to do business in Yellowstone—he would be stuck with two steamboats on Yellowstone Lake and certainly no means to take them elsewhere. That would require hacking them apart, loading the pieces onto horse-drawn wagons again and hauling them north through Yellowstone to the railroad at Gardiner for transport hundreds and hundreds of miles to…where? The Great Lakes? The Puget Sound? The costs would be exorbitant and the prospects dim for a successful venture. He lacked the cash and, by then, the energetic ambition to start over somewhere else. Without a longer lease in Yellowstone or a buyout, his boats and most everything else would be unceremoniously confiscated and Waters would be left with nothing.

So, still weak and recovering from his hospital stay in New York, Waters found himself glumly trying to negotiate the terms of his defeat. In his letter to Cockran, Waters notably failed to mention the raft of complaints filed against the Yellowstone Lake Boat Company through the years and the long-running feud it ran with those in charge of managing the park. Instead, in this narrative he was simply a victim without blame, a weary Civil War veteran trying to keep his family from being destroyed. "We have broken no rules, and in no way had any complaint made against us that we know of," Waters determinedly averred, adding that he could furnish recommendations of thousands of people that his company had "served the traveling public well." [13]

He asked Cockran to appeal to Roosevelt's sense of fairness. "I do not believe that an administration that stands for a 'square deal' when they know fully the situation, will allow this great wrong to be perpetrated," he said, invoking the president's famous vow to treat all fairly.[13]

Cockran agreed. Almost immediately after receiving Waters' letter, he sat down and wrote to his old friend Roosevelt. "Dear Mr. President," it began. "Your love of a square deal which I have appreciated for nearly a generation and which the whole world has learned to admire during the last decade, encourages me to bring before you what I regard as a grave injustice perpetrated—or at least contemplated—by the government through the Interior Department, against a deserving man and a veteran of the Civil War." He detailed Waters' "distressing case" and asked Roosevelt to investigate, using officials wholly unconnected with Yellowstone, the Interior Department, or the railroad company. It was an unusual request, Cockran acknowledged, but one made by "sympathy with an old man" whose "declining years have been clouded by other sorrows."[14]

Roosevelt, in typically impetuous fashion, wrote to Cockran the next day. Yellowstone had been on his mind. Just days before, his old friend John Pitcher—the second-longest-serving superintendent in Yellowstone's brief history—had stepped down and retired from the military. To replace Pitcher, Roosevelt turned to another friend: Samuel Baldwin Marks Young, a retired military general and former chief of staff of the U.S. Army who had served a five-month stint as Yellowstone's superintendent in 1897. "I know but little of Waters, and I am sorry to say that little is to his discredit," Roosevelt said. "Major Pitcher, the later superintendent of the Yellowstone Park, who is certainly a decent and straight man, has recommended that he be put out of the Park."

Roosevelt promised to send Waters' case to Young, calling the new superintendent "a man of rugged independence… [who] can be depended on to do absolutely what he thinks is right without regard to any other consideration." True to his word, later that day Roosevelt's secretary sent a note to Young asking for a report on Waters.[15]

With his trunks barely unpacked in Yellowstone, Young was already getting an earful about the man with the boats on Yellowstone Lake. A visiting surgeon from San Francisco was disgusted by the series of pens and corrals that Waters kept near Lake Hotel for his sheep, elk, bison and horses. The bison, including weeks-old calves, were living in "badly neglected" corrals with no shelter and mud up to two feet deep. The doctor was so troubled by what he saw that he wrote to Young from the Lake Hotel, just hours after his arrival.[16]

The next day, Young dispatched two cavalry officers to investigate. They found eight elk, six bison, sixteen sheep, twenty-three lambs and a half-dozen horses. Almost all of them were living in squalor among filth and mud. "In our opinion," the officers reported back to Young, "this collection of tumbledown huts is, from a sanitary standpoint, a public nuisance." Waters, who remained with his family in Fond du Lac, got word of the complaints by telegram. He told Young that the bison and elk should have been on Dot Island for the summer tourist season by then but that the government had "detained our work." He did not elaborate.[17]

Young asked his officers to investigate other tourist camps and stables around the park. Indeed, several of them were filthy with litter and sewage. A subsequent look at Waters' operations at the Lake Hotel showed no improvement. "The beach adjoining E. C. Waters' concession is very dirty—a refuse and manure heap, in fact. The steamer '*Zillah*' lies beside the wharf with her crew aboard, but the master of the *Zillah* stated to me that he had orders to put her in commission but no orders to make the regular trip," the report said. "He did not know where the owner was."[18]

13 WRECKED

In the summer of 1870, Nathaniel Pitt Langford, who would later become Yellowstone's first superintendent, camped on the shore of Yellowstone Lake along with other members of the famed Washburn expedition and witnessed first-hand its mercurial temperament.

"We have a most beautiful view of the lake from our camp," Langford wrote. "Yesterday it lay before us calm and unruffled, save by the waves which gently broke upon the shore. To-day the winds lash it into a raging sea."[1]

The summer and fall of 1907 was much the same for Waters, now bracing against a sudden and violent shift in conditions from a storm that had been brewing for years. He arrived back in Yellowstone in late June and, just days later, Superintendent Young was fielding more complaints about the boat concessioner and his operations. William Thomas, a visiting lawyer from San Francisco, said he was approached by "a large, elderly man with glasses, with a yachting cap on his head" that he soon learned was Waters trying to drum up business. At the lunch station at Thumb, Waters sat down next to Thomas and began a hard sell to get him to ride the *Zillah*, complaining along the way that the Yellowstone Park Association tried to keep people from riding his boat. Deeply annoyed by the badgering come-on, Thomas stated he would rather take the stagecoach. "In the meantime, I had gone down to the Lake and examined the boat," Thomas said. "It was such an old rattle-trap that I would not risk a passage on it."[2]

With the *Zillah* only limping along now, the *E. C. Waters* made some test runs on the lake. One day in July, passengers were surprised by a soldier in uniform who had been hired by Waters as security aboard his new boat for $15 a month. That day, though, the soldier was armed, drunk and obnoxious. "Quite a number of ladies on the boat were frightened that a man should be on board the boat intoxicated, with a gun in his possession," said one witness. Other soldiers arrested him when the boat reached shore.[3]

Meanwhile at park headquarters in Mammoth, a letter arrived from former Superintendent Frazier Boutelle, who had been kicked out of Yellowstone in 1891 after a run-in with Waters. Boutelle, retired and living in Seattle, was answering a letter from Pitcher, who had apparently written asking about his history with Waters.

Boutelle admitted that he helped to get Waters fired from his job as hotel manager for the Yellowstone Park Association in the late 1880s but said he regretted that he had been unable to stop him from getting the lease for his boat business, "These, I understood have been a graft and a nuisance ever since." It was clear that despite the distance of miles and years, the former superintendent's experience with Waters still grated on him. "I have often thought of the matter and believed if the situation could be brought before the present President, he would make short work of the fellow," Boutelle wrote to Pitcher.[4]

The timing of Boutelle's letter to Mammoth was no accident. That spring and summer Pitcher and Young, the two back-to-back superintendents and both of them Roosevelt friends, were quietly digging up dirt on Waters, no doubt setting the stage for the boat captain's ouster from Yellowstone once and for all. The pair went so far as trying to verify his service in the Civil War, investigating how much land he owned, and how deep in debt he was.[5] A hardware store owner in Red Lodge confirmed that Waters owned eighty acres nearby but had deeded it to one of his other enterprises, the Amory Waters Cattle Company, and had recently bought a ranch.[6] A.L. Babcock, president of the Yellowstone National Bank in Billings, wrote to Pitcher that Waters owned and was assessed for three residential lots in Billings in 1906 but had since transferred them to someone else.[7]

Waters also had debts: $3,500 to a prominent supply company in Billings called Yegen Bros.,[8] and some $1,700 to the W.A. Hall store in Gardiner, a debt Waters had promised that his wife would pay a year earlier as she left Yellowstone through the north entrance. Instead, she exited through the western gate and left the debt unpaid.[9] (The year before, Waters had also been sued by another man for an I.O.U. totaling more than $1,800.[10]) This information gave General Young additional insight into the financial affairs influencing Waters.

The superintendents were also starting to put the squeeze on Waters over his "game show" on Dot Island. "Keeping these animals in captivity is at variance with the spirit of having this greatest of all national parks maintain with the fidelity the original conditions of Nature as far as possible," Young said in early August 1907. Even at this early date a philosophy of allowing nature to take its normal course was evolving in Yellowstone.[11]

A week later, a group of game wardens visited Dot Island, another episode that seems to have been more than mere happenstance in a possible drive to eject Waters. The National Association of Game and Fish Wardens and Commissioners was formed in 1902 on the outskirts of Yellowstone National Park. In the summer of 1907, Pitcher was serving on the group's board of directors and its president was W.F. Scott, the Montana game warden who, several years earlier, relayed to his old friend Pitcher the vitriol that Waters spewed about him during a ride on the *Zillah*. Now here they were visiting Waters' operation on Dot Island—and indeed riding Waters' own *Zillah* to get there.

"When we landed at Dot Island for the purpose of seeing the elk and buffalo confined there, I was one of the last to land, and, while going across the gang plank, my attention was attracted by a nauseating and sour smell," Scott wrote to Young in a letter of complaint. "Upon looking around I saw a deck hand following me, carrying two buckets of the vilest smelling slop or swill." [12]

The buckets contained food for Waters' captive and increasingly pathetic elk. "When we reached the corral this repugnant mess was poured out into a trough where these poor emaciated creatures, driven to desperation by hunger, fought for an opportunity to eat at the trough, where, for the first time in my life, I saw elk eat flesh," Scott said, adding that he watched a cow elk take a piece of meat to the other side of the corral where she devoured it "like a dog." Scott's letter, written on the group's official stationery, concluded by saying he was repulsed to know that hundreds of tourists witnessed "this inhuman sight" every day and that he was hereby protesting "in the name of humanity." [12]

Meanwhile, a top-ranking wildlife official with the U.S.

Department of Agriculture, T.S. Palmer, was also present on the Dot Island trip, and he, too, complained to Young about the starving elk and buffalo. "The filthy corrals, the noisome odors and the sight of elk fed like hogs on stale garbage disgusted several of the passengers," Thomas said. Feed them properly, he declared, or release them.[13]

Young told Waters that "many good people" had complained about the elk and bison on the island and that he was therefore immediately shutting it down for good. He ordered all the animals to be taken away by the end of the tourist season.[14]

Predictably Waters adamantly refused to give up on Dot Island or his steamers. Nothing about his lease had yet been resolved but he was nevertheless investing heavily in his new steamboat. His one-time enemy with the federal Steamboat Inspection Service, John Sloan (whom he had tried to get fired in 1891), had been out to Yellowstone in July and spent two days inspecting the *Zillah* and *E. C. Waters*. Sloan left a long list of suggested improvements for both vessels, including a heater for the newer ship and better safety equipment for the *Zillah*. Waters moved quickly to get them installed, although he mentioned later that he planned to phase out the *Zillah's* role in moving passengers on the lake. The *E. C. Waters*, acknowledged by the inspector that it was allowed to carry up to six hundred passengers, represented Waters' future. "She handles like a duck and every one is more than pleased," Waters told Sloan.[15]

With the larger ship still mostly idle, the *Zillah* remained the tenacious queen of the lake that summer, carrying a record 5,275 passengers. One of them late that summer of 1907 was William Howard Taft, the Secretary of War whom Roosevelt had hand-picked to be his successor in the White

House. Waters predictably took the opportunity to plead his case to the rising political star, who was visiting Yellowstone with his wife, and to launch more bitter complaints against his enemies, including Harry Child.[16]

"I remember thinking that there was room enough in the Park for Waters and Child," Taft recalled about his conversation with Waters.[17]

Even so, the end had almost certainly been written for Waters by then. The summer season closed in September. As Waters and his crew again went out to Dot Island to retrieve their elk and bison, he must have known the tide was turning against him. Before the 1907 summer tourist season began, park officials told him that, at the end of the year, he would no longer be allowed to keep the animals in his pen near the Lake Hotel. Now with the season shutting down, Waters' lawyer sent a letter proposing to sell four bison and six elk to the government—animals that had come from outside the park—for the suggested price of $6,000 plus a lease on some nearby land outside of Yellowstone.

Young, the superintendent, knew the wretched conditions those animals had been living in, sometimes wallowing in their own dung and urine. He also knew that they would be more trouble than they were worth so he urged his government bosses in Washington to reject the offer and to permit him to drive Waters' animals out of Yellowstone for good. Young, self-assured like his friend Roosevelt, did not wait for a reply from his higher-ups. Waters closed up his Yellowstone business for the year on September 22 and left the park, and the next day, Young wrote him to see if he planned to comply with the order to remove his corrals and the bison and elk. Three days later Waters' response arrived, telling Pitcher that he had no intention of taking down the corrals or moving the animals.[18]

With tourists finally gone and the chill of fall setting in, a crew personally supervised by Superintendent Young arrived at Lake Hotel on a Tuesday in mid-October and tore down Waters' corrals. Seven elk and eight bison suddenly ran free into Yellowstone. (For several years these bison—which were originally part of the Goodnight herd of Texas and never part of Yellowstone's native herds—roamed the park on their own. Several were rounded up in December 1909 at Lake to be driven toward Mammoth in chest-deep snow. They broke free, however, and died one by one through the years.)

The day after the corrals came down at Lake, on October 16, 1907, Superintendent Young issued this public bulletin:

> NOTICE! E. C. Waters, president of the Yellowstone Lake Boat Company, having rendered himself obnoxious during the season of 1907, is, under the provisions of paragraph 11, Rules and Regulations of Yellowstone National Park, debarred from the Park and will not be allowed to return without permission in writing from the Secretary of the Interior or the Superintendent of the Park. Young. [19]

So, that was it for Waters. He had finally been kicked out of Yellowstone, the place where he and his family spent every summer for two decades. Waters had lost and the system that he felt was rigged against him from the start had won. This could not have been terribly surprising to E. C. Waters; after all, he had been on the verge of expulsion numerous times through many years. But here—suddenly arriving like the burst of a shell—came a sense of finality that must have shocked him, at least initially.

Like a wounded animal refusing to die, Waters quickly set

aside his hurt and shame and focused on trying to find some way to salvage something, anything, from his troubled and rapidly failing business. He had already been shamed and ostracized; surely he could secure some kind of financial compensation that would wash some of the sour out of his mouth.

Within weeks of being kicked out of Yellowstone, Waters cast about to his network of connections for anyone who might want to buy the Yellowstone Lake Boat Company. If he really was expelled from Yellowstone, he at least wanted to get paid on his way out the door. All of the physical property related to his company—from the *Zillah* and the *E. C. Waters* to rowboats, fishing poles, tools and the blacksmith shop—were worth about $200,000, he figured. Then there were some rather intangible values, such as the leases and "good will," appraisals that were difficult to calculate for someone with Waters' troubled history. Probably gritting his teeth, he estimated that the entire value of his Yellowstone business was about $300,000.[20]

Rather than returning to Fond du Lac at the end of his final tourist season, Waters stayed near the park in Livingston, licking his wounds and likely assuming that the next few months would be crucial to his financial future. By early December, a company acting as a middleman told him it had found someone willing to buy the business for $250,000 in cash—but only if it came with a ten- or twenty-year lease and a guarantee that no competing company be allowed to operate steamboats or rowboats on the lake.[20] And if that could not happen, the buyer must be allowed to operate hotels and transportation in the park, a stipulation that was highly unlikely given the tight grip that the Northern Pacific Railway and its subsidiaries still had on Yellowstone's hotels.

Waters returned to Fond du Lac and stewed over the offer.

In January 1908, he wrote a letter to Interior Secretary Garfield on letterhead from the "Temporary office of the Yellowstone Lake Boat Company" in Wisconsin. He included his middleman's note about the potential buyer but, true to his sense of paranoia and his believed persecution from enemies far and wide, declined to reveal their names. "I am afraid that if I do that inside of 48 hours (as I know has been the case heretofore) the said information will be conveyed to those that have been and are now doing all they can to accomplish this company's financial ruin," said Waters. "We have no preference as to who buys our plant so long as it is satisfactory to the government and we get our money." [20]

Most of Waters' letter to the Secretary was mundanely businesslike, enumerating down to the penny all of the company's expenditures for that year and its net earnings. The profits that summer, after hefty operating expenses, amounted to a meager $74.19. Midway through the letter, however, Waters drifted into a rambling bit of desperation and melancholy.

> For twenty-one years the Park has been the home of the majority stockholders of the Boat Co. Their children have been raised there. It is the place that has been called home to them for that time, the place where the cool, dry crisp and bracing mountain air keeps them in good health in their declining years, the one place on earth where they had hoped to spend their summers as long as they lived, and at the end of life hand over to their children an established business—a business that they had built up and undertaken when others refused to attempt it, a business the Government urged them to undertake, and a business

that 98 per cent of the traveling public will say has
been well and properly conducted in their interests, a
business under our management that during the past
eighteen seasons has never had an accident or injured
a passenger although during that time we have carried
nearly if not more than 52,361 passengers.[20]

Unbeknownst to Waters, by the time his letter reached
Secretary Garfield's desk in Washington, it was already too
late. Less than a month after Young expelled Waters, the
Interior Department secured a new agreement for boat op-
erations on the lake with a longtime Yellowstone guide, T.E.
"Billy" Hofer, as owner and manager.

The deal, reached in November 1907 and finalized in early
1908, contracted Hofer's company for ten years of boating
services on Yellowstone Lake, including ten motor boats and
up to fifty rowboats. The original deal, representing an extra "twist of the knife" for Waters, also leased out the long
wooden docks near the Lake Hotel that Waters had built and
even the lakeside house that he and his family had spent so
many summers in.

As his boat company collapsed, so did Waters' physical
health. Back in Wisconsin, he became seriously ill and soon
found himself at the Tuberculosis and Consumption Sanatorium. [21] The state-run facility, which had opened just a few
months earlier, was designed for patients with "incipient and
moderately advanced cases"[22] of tuberculosis, which, along
with pneumonia, was the leading cause of death in the U.S.
at the time.[23]

He was in bad shape. If his case was typical, as the tuberculosis attacked his lungs, his breathing became labored. He
likely became tired, prone to eruptive coughing fits, exasper-

ated, and near comatose. His brother, Homer, had suffered the same way before he died in Billings nearly twenty years earlier. Waters was supposed to rest at the sanatorium but in lucid moments his troubled mind, almost certainly, found its way back to Yellowstone, his vanishing enterprise, and the *E. C. Waters*—fully appointed and finally completed but anchored uselessly at Stevenson Island. Everything was falling apart for him.

With her husband fifty miles away in the sanatorium, Waters' wife Martha settled in at Fond du Lac and dutifully tried to salvage the pieces of the Yellowstone Lake Boat Company. The boat business was gone, that much was clear, but they still had money tied up in the groceries and other goods at the little store they ran near the Lake Hotel. As spring turned to summer, Martha Waters, "in great distress," asked the Yellowstone superintendent if she and Waters, once he was well enough to travel again, could return to the park to sell their last remaining goods to the tourists that summer. Waters' biting sense of injustice had rubbed off on his wife—their ouster from Yellowstone was still an open wound for them both. "We are thrust aside," Martha pleaded to the superintendent's office, "and our life's earnings taken from us."[24]

Park officials refused Martha's request. Superintendent Young, suspicious as ever, figured Waters was angling "toward perpetuating his stay in the park." Instead, the government gave Waters permission only to come to Yellowstone, collect anything that was his that had not been sold to Hofer, and leave again.[25]

Summer and fall came and went and Waters never materialized. His disruptive presence was still felt, however: At the height of the tourist season, one of the ornery old bison that had been released from Water's corrals ran loose near Fishing

Bridge, "disturbing traffic and endangering the lives of tourists by frightening horses etc along the stage road."[26]

Meanwhile Young, the superintendent who had finally succeeded in expelling Waters from Yellowstone, left his job at Mammoth on November 28, 1908. He was replaced by Harry Benson, an intellectual soldier and administrator and a veteran of the Apache Indian wars who most recently had served as a provost marshal in San Francisco while the city was under martial law in the wake of the 1906 fire.[27]

Benson, no doubt briefed on Waters' situation, wasted little time in going after him. That winter, he ordered members of the cavalry to seize everything Waters had left behind at Lake, including many of the items that Martha Waters had hoped to sell the previous summer, among them nineteen cans of beans; sixteen pounds of butter; forty-nine pounds of coffee; three hundred fifty pounds of flour; miscellaneous plates, bowls, and door mats; a lemon squeezer; and ten water pitchers. There were also personal effects left behind: a croquet set, a piano, a violin, items that no doubt found their uses around the Waters' family home during evenings in Yellowstone after the *Zillah* was docked for the day.[28]

Despite his sickness, Waters fought on in a last-ditch attempt to salvage something from his unfolding disaster in Yellowstone. He fell in with another politically connected Republican attorney, Ohio's Arthur I. Vorys, who just happened to be one of the campaign managers for William Howard Taft during his successful run for president in 1908. Waters' arm-twisting on his new friend worked—to a degree. Taft was in the White House less than three months when he wrote to his new Interior secretary, Richard Ballinger, to say that his "warm and intimate friend" Vorys had relayed complaints from Waters and that Harry Child had "been de-

voting a great deal of attention to attacking and undermin-
ing" him. "I hope you will give Mr. Vorys an opportunity to
discuss the matter and tell him as much as you know or can
find out in respect to this situation," Taft wrote in June 1909,
"and can enable him to secure justice for Waters, whatever
that may be."[29]

In July, Vorys also wrote Superintendent Benson asking
to see record books from the Yellowstone Lake Boat Company, and noting that he had just talked with Waters, who
said his wife's health was now suddenly failing. "I suspect
his fears about this wife's serious condition are only too well
founded," Vorys said. "It seems to me he has about as much
of this world's misfortunes to contend with as any man I ever
met. I am still all worked up about him."[30]

Less than three weeks later, Martha was dead of cancer in
Fond du Lac. She was only fifty-five.[31]

Again, Waters found himself in the grips of grief and further loss just as his affairs in Yellowstone were in incredible
flux. With his wife and youngest daughter gone, and his oldest daughter off and married, only his twenty-one-year-old
son Amory remained with him. And yet, Waters, now sixty
and buffeted by age, illness, and years of conflict in the park,
refused again to simply give up on Yellowstone.

Oddly, Taft's interest and Vorys' influence had begun to
pay off. In particular, the Interior Department was warming
to Waters' relentless argument that, according to a provision
in his earlier contract, the government had the option to either pay him for the improvements he made to the park—like
construction of the boat docks—or extend his boating lease
for another ten years. In September 1909, Interior Secretary
Ballinger in Washington, D.C., told Benson at Yellowstone
that Waters was expected to return to the park to prepare

some of his boats, those apparently not sold to Hofer, for winter. Ballinger asked Benson if Waters' workers could stay at the military station at Lake. Benson declined, first saying there was not enough food or space, then adding that some of the supplies were available only through credit, "and from Mr Waters' known financial actions, he would not be likely to pay if he were trusted."[32]

Word began to trickle out that Waters might be making a last desperate play to permanently return to Yellowstone. Even former Superintendent Young, who was back in Washington in a new job presiding over a board of inquiry about a soldiers' riot in 1906, had heard. He quickly fired off a note to Benson, the new superintendent. "Dame rumor says that Waters is again to be given a concession under contract to run his boats on the Yellowstone Lake," a disgusted Young wrote. "The return of Waters to the park would be a serious reflection on my administration of affairs in the park....Waters has always been a disgrace to the Park and is a dangerous bad man."[33]

An unsigned response to Young marked "confidential" at the top—and almost certainly from Benson—confirmed that it seemed true, that Waters was again to be given a contract. The Taft administration apparently felt like it was on the losing end of Waters' legal strategy and that they were left with either paying him for all of his property and improvements at Yellowstone or extending his lease for another decade. The Taft White House and the Interior Department were fully aware "of the undesirability of this man," the letter said, but felt "constrained, under the law, to renew his permit."[34]

Regardless of "dame rumor," it still seemed unlikely to many that Waters would ever return to operate the boats on Yellowstone Lake, the letter-writer assured Young. "We certainly would be mighty glad to be rid of Waters and all his tribe. The only way it seems likely to get rid of him is to authorize a competing company, and let Waters die of starvation," wrote Benson.[34]

Just a few weeks later, at the end of May 1910, Interior Secretary Ballinger penned a detailed, six-page letter to President Taft outlining the situation with Waters in Yellowstone. Yes, Waters' Yellowstone Lake Boat Company could get a contract. But Waters himself, by order of the government, "shall be eliminated from any connection with the operation of the company in the park."[35]

Within months, Waters had sold most of his remaining equipment to Hofer. Hunkered down in Fond du Lac, he was still not well. He nonetheless wanted to return to Yellowstone one more time to retrieve a few remaining pieces of equipment that did not get sold to Hofer. "My health is such that it may be impossible for me to go there at present," Waters wrote to Benson, asking permission to send two of his remaining employees instead.[36]

Benson agreed and, by fall 1910, most, but not all, of Waters' provisions at Lake were gone. "There are still two domestic sheep running at large in the vicinity of the Lake Outlet that formerly belonged to the Yellowstone Lake Boat Company," Benson said as cold weather set in with another summer tourist season past. "These sheep have become rather wild, and being old are of little value, and it is doubtful if Mr. Waters expects to claim them."[37]

Ballinger had the final say on Waters' long and troubled tenure in Yellowstone and the reason why he had to go: "His incompatibility."[38]

14 CAST AWAY

Waters never did return to Yellowstone to run his boat company. He was finally gone and certainly those who ran the park were glad of it. Hofer ran the boats, including the *Zillah*, but was never able to do much with them. After a series of complicated transactions, the boat company came under control of Waters' old nemesis, Harry Child. Even under Child's shrewd eye for business, the boat company still only limped along. When automobiles finally arrived in Yellowstone in 1915, the park changed forever. Boats were fun, but cars were better.[1]

The ultimate fate of the *Zillah* remains unclear, even after many years of park personnel and others searching for it. It was "an old rattletrap" by the early 1900s and only deteriorated from there. By the time Child bought the boat company, the *Zillah* was out of commission. It became a ghost of history after that. It showed up in one photo from the 1920s, perched high and dry on the shore at Lake near one of its successors, the *Jean D*, but then largely disappeared from history.

Some said the *Zillah* was eventually towed out, purposefully punctured and jettisoned to the bottom of the lake. Others claim it was pulled apart and cannibalized for scrap. Either way was an ignominious end for a ship that turned out to be a stalwart and long-lived workhorse for Waters on Yellowstone Lake. Was anyone sad to see it vanish? Would anyone remember the tens of thousands of passengers it carried or the peculiar sight of it towing a barge full of bison and elk back and forth to Dot Island? The steel-hulled boat once called *Useless* had indeed faithfully fulfilled its duties for more than two decades in Yellowstone.[2]

The *E. C. Waters* was another story. It almost certainly never carried a paying passenger. Though it was far more elegant than the *Zillah*, the *E. C. Waters* was ultimately defined by its utter futility, an expensive promise unfulfilled—and, of course, an unmistakable, even garish, reminder of the most hated businessman in Yellowstone. When Waters left Yellowstone, the *E. C. Waters* remained in the middle of Yellowstone Lake, moored in a cove on the east side of Stevenson Island. The sandy inlet was supposed to be safe from the lake ice that accumulated every winter and broke up each spring; typically a southwestern wind kept any ice away from the ship. But in the spring of 1921, as the frozen lake was breaking up, stiff winds from the east drove the ice—and the *E. C. Waters*— into the island, hoisting the massive ship awkwardly onto the beach and depositing it on its side, leaving its port side partially submerged and its starboard flank vulnerably exposed.

Men with tools descended on the derelict ship. The engine and much of the machinery were removed. The biggest prize was the twelve-foot Scotch boiler —the wood-burning monster that gave the *E. C. Waters* its power. Crews from the Lake Hotel pulled it out in 1926, no small chore given island's remote location and the ship's precarious positioning, and hauled it back to the great lakeside hotel. For the next forty-six years, the boiler that was supposed to run Waters' mighty dream of a ship was used instead to heat the Lake Hotel and the very halls that Waters, once upon a time, stalked in search of customers for his beleaguered business.

On Stevenson Island, the remaining hulk of the *E. C. Waters* began a second career as a wrecked curiosity and meeting spot for those in the know. In the winter, skiers on the lake huddled for warmth in the shelter of the abandoned ship. A businessman named Jack Croney (ironically, an employee of a later iteration of the Yellowstone Lake Boat Company) used the wreckage as site for regular fish fries. It also became popular for drunken parties and "brawls fueled by moonshine" by park and concession employees, often at night and out of sight of the visiting public.[3]

Through time, the wreck became part of the local lore for visitors on the lake; tour guides were too happy for many years to supply a mocking story of Waters' folly. "We have people from every state stop and ask about the old boat at the Island," Croney once said. "Their friends have told them to be sure and don't pass the Lake without first taking a boat over and have the laugh of their lives."[4]

The park had become a different place since Waters left. The National Park Service, created in 1916, took over management of the park from the military. Yellowstone was becoming known world-wide and held up as a model for how national parks should be run—orderly and carefully controlled. But for some park rangers, the derelict ship on Stevenson Island, and the delinquent behavior it too often hosted, had become too much to tolerate. In the fall of 1930, rangers stationed at Lake began a campaign of cleaning up unsightly buildings left over from Yellowstone's wilder and woollier days. They removed or burned cabins, sheds, barns, old tent frames, and horse racks. Then someone mentioned the wreck of the *E. C. Waters*. Why not burn that old bag of bones, too?

"The main reason [to burn it] would be abolishing of wild drinking orgies or parties carried out on Stevenson Island on this beached boat by members of the Boat Company, and employees of the Hotel Company," said Assistant Ranger E.E. "Ted" Ogston, who was in charge of the Lake Ranger Station. "The boat was an eye sore."[5]

In January 1931, with ice thick on top of Yellowstone Lake, two park rangers—Albert Elliot and Skeet Dart—along with hotel winter-keeper "Boots" Chenard skied out to the wreck, doused the bow with kerosene, and lit it. The fire, despite a plume of black smoke swirling into the wintry sky, ultimately did only minimal damage to the stubborn wreck.[6]

But back at Yellowstone headquarters in Mammoth, the news caused a firestorm. Jack Croney lit into his boss, William Nichols, at the Yellowstone Lake Boat Company, confused and angered by the burning. To him, the *E. C. Waters* had become an important tourist stop, including for those taking a one-hour joy ride around the lake in the company's smaller boats. "You can figure on at least 15 or 20 percent of the Boat Co. receipts shot on that deal," Croney railed in a letter. "Don't know what we will do now for a talking point." Croney ranted on, complaining that the company should have been warned about plans to burn the ship so they could salvage what they wanted. "I hope you can give someone hell for it," he told his boss. "I'm all burned up about it."[7]

Nichols, surprised to learn about what had happened, complained to Yellowstone headquarters and the Department of the Interior. Guy Edwards, the acting superintendent in Mammoth, offered a bureaucrat's apology: "We regret very much the burning of the boat and that it was burned without permission from the office."[8]

Ogston, the leader of the Lake rangers but not present when the boat was burned, was called to Mammoth for a dressing-down. He was charged with destroying the boat company's property and told to make a $500 restitution payment. Ogston willingly took his lumps to protect his rangers, even though he could have easily passed the buck and blamed them.[9] He paid the fine himself but disputed claims that the wreck was somehow a moneymaker. "Jack Croney was the main person effected [sic] by the loss of this boat and I expected he would complain to Mr. Nichols," Ogston said. "It is untrue that a large revenue is received from a trip to the boat, for Lake Yellowstone carries beauty elsewhere."[10]

The park rangers kept their jobs: Elliot eventually became superintendent at Mount Rushmore National Monument and Ogston the chief ranger at Death Valley, after a punishment-stint at the Statue of Liberty National Monument.

The *E. C. Waters* remained on Stevenson Island, weathering unending waves and the lake's freezing-thawing cycles each winter and spring. Waters himself did not last as long as his monumental boat. Although he was banned from Yellowstone, Waters maintained connections in Montana and Wyoming, where he invested in coal, livestock and mining. His daughter, Edna, who had run off to marry the Lake Hotel clerk, had died in 1913. Waters' only remaining family, son Amory, appears to have stayed in Montana. Waters survived his bout with the tuberculosis that put him into the sanatorium and resettled back home, first in Fond du Lac and then, as his health worsened and his mind decayed, spent his final chapter quietly—far away from controversy and consternation and Yellowstone—in Waupaca at the Wisconsin Veterans Home.

After a long illness, E. C. Waters died on August 18, 1926, at the age of seventy-seven. The news made the front page of the paper in Fond du Lac, noting that he was a Civil War veteran and "known for his large and successful enterprises in western states." His time in Yellowstone warranted but two paragraphs in the eleven-paragraph story. There was no mention of his troubles there. He was buried two days later with a delegation from the local Grand Army of the Republic attending. Sadly, news reports did not say whether his son, Amory, or any other family, attended.[11]

Word of Waters' death reached Yellowstone's headquarters at Mammoth that fall. Although a long succession of superintendents would have been happy to forget Waters and all the heartburn he produced in more than two decades in the park, Superintendent Horace Albright wrote to the soldiers' home asking if Waters had left any books or papers that might be shipped to Yellowstone. For good or ill, Albright understood Waters was part of the park's complicated, colorful history. "While I never knew Colonel Waters," Albright said in the letter that was eventually returned to sender, "he was quite a character here in the old days."[12]

Though Yellowstone consumed his heart and mind for much of his life, in his final days Waters apparently had no memory of ever being in the park—captaining the *Zillah*, building the *E. C. Waters*, or fighting his ceaseless wars with the military, the railroad, Harry Child, and Theodore Roosevelt's powerful friends. His mind, according to one report, was "entirely gone."[12]

EPILOGUE

The skeleton of the *E. C. Waters* remains on Stevenson Island, a bull-headed beast unmoved by the years. This author visited it on a near-perfect morning in early August of 2012. The boat is right where Waters abandoned it, listing on its port side, partially submerged in the sand, slowly disintegrating against the ceaseless grind of Yellowstone's seasons.

It is strange to touch a piece of history. You think it is going to feel different, that the wood is going to feel like more than just wood, that there will be some kind of electrical current that connects you with the past. But what was once the source of such pride and aggravation is now simply a failing collection of weathered timbers and rusting bolts. Gone are the brass handles that Waters picked out, the delicate doorknobs, the perfect glass panes that would be the passengers' windows to the amazing world of Yellowstone Lake.

What is left is a gray skeleton, deprived of the obvious signs of life that it once promised. A closer inspection, though, reveals much more. In 1996, the National Park Service sent a team of archeologists to Stevenson Island. They spent five summer days documenting every inch of the wreck, often submerged in frigid waters in wetsuits and SCUBA gear. They drew up meticulous and painfully constructed maps, like a crime scene, and produced lengthy explanations of each piece and speculation about how the boat had been put together and torn apart. They counted the boards used for the boat's frame and measured them down to the quarter-inch. They discussed the pattern used to attach fasteners in the stern, as well as the bearing and bushing assembly. We know the *E. C. Waters* had seven davits, those hook-shaped devices used to lift lifeboats and ladders, and that the total length of propeller system, from the crankshaft coupling to the far end of the propeller hub, was precisely 37 feet, 10.5 inches.

I thought about those scuba-diving researchers while I walked around the *E. C. Waters* that morning. This ship— and, more to the point, the man responsible for it—had been discarded to history at one time, left to rot and forever disappear from view. *Good-bye and good riddance* was the sentiment voiced by more than a few. Time, though, had reversed all that. At some point, who knows when, the *E. C. Waters* became valuable again. No longer a derelict, it was an archeological artifact to be studied, analyzed and dissected. For those of us in the modern world, the wreck became a strange window into so many facets of a time and place gone by: the first years of Yellowstone, shipbuilding techniques, early tourism, and even the nation's battle for the soul of the Gilded Age.

I was happy to know that so much effort had been put into cataloguing every inch of the wreck and could not help but wonder what Waters would think of it all. He would love that such a fuss was still being made over his ship and that, nearly a century after he left it on Stevenson Island, it survived. His house next to the Lake Hotel is long gone now—it is just a patch of ground covered in shrubs and grasses and new trees—as is the town of Cinnabar, where the *Zillah* first arrived by train, creating a spectacle. The giant boiler yanked out of the *E. C. Waters* and put to work to heat the Lake Hotel was carted away to a landfill in the 1970s. The lakeside docks where people once lined up to board have disappeared, too.

A few remnants of the ship now linger on the mainland. Someone once tried to steal the capstan from the wreck but failed. In the late 1990s, Park Historian Lee Whittlesey and former Lake District Ranger John Lounsbury took it from the wreck (others recovered a porthole and the boat's anchor) and placed them safely in storage in a government building near Gardiner. The anchor is now on display at Bridge Bay Marina. The bulk of the wreck has stayed on the island, though, outlasting friends, enemies and even a fire meant to destroy it once and for all.

While I was on Stevenson Island, the modern iteration of the *E. C. Waters*—the shiny, sleek forty-four-foot *Lake Queen II*, capable of carrying forty passengers on an hour-long tour of Yellowstone Lake—pulled up next to the wreck and let its engine idle. Inside, I could see the silhouettes of curious travelers shifting in their seats to get a better view of the defeated wreckage. I imagined the stories the tour guide was telling about E. C. Waters and wondered whether those visitors were laughing or just pitying this man who had done so much to derail his own dreams, which included running "the finest craft afloat between the Great Lakes and the Puget Sound."

The *Lake Queen* stayed for just a few minutes before motoring away. I left shortly after. The *E. C. Waters* remained, as it had for so long: tireless against the waves lapping at its bones.

CHAPTER NOTES

Correspondence, reports, and other documents from the era when the United States Army administered Yellowstone National Park (1886-1918), referred to below simply as "Army Records," are housed in the Yellowstone National Park Archives, Gardiner, Montana. Many other resources were also used in researching the current volume.

PROLOGUE

1. Jack Croney to W.M. Nichols, May 23, 1931, Yellowstone National Park Archives, Gardiner, MT.

CHAPTER 1

1. "The New Boat Launched," *Wonderland* (Gardiner, MT, newspaper), September 21, 1905, 1.

2. E. C. Waters to undisclosed recipients, January 18, 1905, Army Records.

3. "The New Boat Launched."

4. W.S. Rossington to Assistant Secretary of the Interior Thomas Ryan, July 26, 1902, Army Records.

5. Acting Superintendent John Pitcher to the Secretary of the Interior, June 6, 1903, Army Records.

6. Letters among Harry Child (July 22, 1904), F. Jay Haynes (July 24, 1904), and Superintendent Pitcher (July 25, 1904), Army Records.

CHAPTER 2

1. Helen Fitzgerald Sanders, *A History of Montana*, Vol. II (Chicago: Lewis Publishing Company, 1913), 918-22.

2. Maurice McKenna, ed., *Fond du Lac County, Wisconsin, Past and Present*, Vol. 2 (Chicago: The S.J. Clarke Publishing Company, 1912), 450-55.

3. Ibid.

4. Sanders.

5. McKenna.

6. Sanders.

7. Ibid.

8. Department of Montana, Grand Army of the Republic, *Proceedings, First, Second, Third and Fourth Encampments, 1885, 1886, 1887, 1888* (Helena, MT: Fisk Brothers, Printers and Binders, 1888), 47. Google Books scanned ed., accessed via The New York Public Library, 777854.

9. Information on Waters, after the Civil War through his marriage, from Sanders.

10. Rocky Barker, *Scorched Earth: How the Fires of Yellowstone Changed America* (Washington, DC: Island Press, 2005), 46.

11. Michael A. Leeson, *History of Montana*, 1739-1885 (Chicago: Warner, Beers, 1885), 547

12. Sanders.

13. Leeson, *History of Montana*, 1056.

14. *Daily Yellowstone Journal* (Miles City, MT), "Montana Mention," March 18, 1885, 1.

15. Sanders.

16. E.V. Smalley, "The New North-west," Century Illustrated

Monthly, Vol. 24, May-September 1882, 69.

17. Carroll Van West, *Capitalism on the Frontier: Billings and the Yellowstone Valley in the Nineteenth Century* (Lincoln: University of Nebraska Press, 1993), 121, Google ed.

18. *Daily Yellowstone Journal* (Miles City, MT), April 4, 1886, 3.

19. Indiana Historical Society, "Biographical Sketch," Russell B. Harrison Collection, 1880-1908, Manuscripts and Archives Department, Indianapolis, accessed at http://www.indianahistory.org/our-collections/collection-guides/russell-b-harrison-collection-1880-1908.pdf.

20. F.A. Boutelle to Major Pitcher, June 15, 1907, Army Records.

CHAPTER 3

1. Aubrey L. Haines, *The Yellowstone Story*, Vol. 2 (Boulder: Yellowstone Library and Museum Association and Colorado Associated University Press, 1977), 449.

2. John L. Stoddard, John L. Stoddard's Lectures: Southern California, Grand Canon of the Colorado River, Yellowstone National Park (Boston: Balch Brothers, 1898), 208-09.

3. The story of Yellowstone's earliest inhabitants is in Aubrey L. Haines, *The Yellowstone Story*, Vol. 1 (Boulder: Yellowstone Library and Museum Association and Colorado Associated University Press, 1977), 15-33.

4. Secretary of the Interior Columbus Delano to Hayden, May 1, 1871, quoted in Aubrey L. Haines, *Yellowstone National Park: Its Exploration and Establishment* (Washington, DC: U.S. Department of the Interior, National Park Service, 1974), Part II, accessed via http://www.nps.gov/parkhistory/online_books/haines1/index.htm

5. The story of Yellowstone's geological past is well-told in Robert B. Smith and Lee J. Siegel, *Windows into the Earth: The Geological Story of Yellowstone and Grand Teton National Parks* (New York: Oxford University Press, 2000).

6. Mark H. Bunnell, in his report from the Committee on Public Lands, U.S. House of Representatives, January 27, 1872, quoted

in F.V. Hayden, *Preliminary Report of the United States Geological Survey of Montana and Portions of Adjacent Territories, Being a Fifth Annual Report of Progress* (Washington, DC: Government Printing Office, 1872). Accessed via Google Books, University of California, Berkeley, Department of Geology and Mineralogy.

7. This topic is thoroughly covered in Paul Schullery and Lee Whittlesey, *Myth and History in the Creation of Yellowstone National Park* (Lincoln: University of Nebraska Press, 2003).

8. Haines, *Yellowstone Story*, Vol. 2, 449.

9. William Gilpin, in a report to the U.S. Senate, 1846, as quoted in Chris J. Magoc, *So Glorious a Landscape: Nature and the Environment in American History and Culture* (Wilmington, DE: Scholarly Resources, Inc., 2002), 43.

10. Matthew A. Russell, James E. Bradford, and Larry E. Murphy, "E. C. Waters and Development of a Turn-of-the Century Economy in Yellowstone National Park," *Historical Archaeology*, 2004, Vol. 38, No. 4, 96-113.

11. Richard A. Bartlett, "The Concessionaires of Yellowstone National Park: Genesis of a Policy, 1882-1892," *Pacific Northwest Quarterly*, January 1983, Vol. 74, No. 1, 2-10.

12. Haines, *Yellowstone Story* Vol. 2, 31.

13. For the $1 million construction cost, see testimony of Thomas F. Oakes, president of the Northern Pacific Railway Company, May 13, 1892, to the Committee on Public Lands, quoted in the committee's "Inquiry into the Management and Control of the Yellowstone National Park," 52nd Congress, House of Representatives, 1st Session, Report No. 1956, United States Congressional Serial Set, SN-3051 (Washington, DC: Government Printing Office), 228. Google Books, accessed via University of California, Davis, library.

14. Richard A. Bartlett, "The Concessionaires," 2-10.

15. Haines, *Yellowstone Story*, Vol. 2, 31.

16. *New York Times*, quoted in Bartlett, "Concessionaires," 4-5.

17. Bartlett, "Concessionaires," 5.

18. Chris J. Magoc, *Yellowstone: The Creation and Selling of an American Landscape*, 1870-1903 (Albuquerque: University of New

Mexico Press, 1999), 62.

19. Haines, *Yellowstone Story*, Vol. 2, 33.

20. Magoc, *Creation and Selling*, 62.

21. Magoc, *Creation and Selling*, 76; Haines, *Yellowstone Story*, Vol. 2, 478.

22. Cartoon from *Harper's Weekly* as reproduced in Magoc, *Creation and Selling*, 66.

23. Quoted in Bartlett, "Concessionaires," 7.

24. Vest quoted in Magoc, *Creation and Selling*, 63.

25. Kansas Sen. John J. Ingalls, quoted in Magoc, *Creation and Selling*, 62.

26. Superintendent Patrick Conger quoted in Magoc, *Creation and Selling*,75.

27. Haines, *Yellowstone Story*, Vol. 2, 42-44.

28. Gibson quoted in Bartlett, "Concessionaires," 8.

29. Testimony of Oakes, in "Inquiry," SN-3051, 228.

CHAPTER 4

1. "The National Park Hotel System," *Daily Yellowstone Journal* (Miles City, MT), April 22, 1887, 3.

2. "Col. E. C. Waters Talks of Proposed Improvements at the National Park," *St. Paul (MN) Daily Globe*, March 7, 1888, 2.

3. Quoted in Paul Schullery, *Searching for Yellowstone: Ecology and Wonder in the Last Wilderness* (Helena: Montana Historical Society Press, 2004), 97.

4. Merrill D. Beal, *The Story of Man in Yellowstone* (Yellowstone Park, WY: The Yellowstone Library and Museum Association, 1956), 245.

5. Quoted in Beal, 262.

6. Department of Montana, Grand Army of the Republic, *Proceedings, First, Second, Third and Fourth Encampments, 1885, 1886, 1887, 1888* (Helena, MT: Fisk Brothers, Printers and Binders, 1888), 47. Google Books scanned ed., accessed via New York Public Library, 777854.

7. Quoted in James R. Heintze, *The Fourth of July Encyclopedia* (Jefferson, N.C., McFarland & Company, Inc., 2007), 324 (accessed via Google Books).

8. Aubrey L. Haines, *The Yellowstone Story*, Vol. 2 (Boulder: Yellowstone Library and Museum Association and Colorado Associated University Press, 1977), 18.

9. "Montana and General," *Philipsburg (MT) Mail*, July 12, 1888, 4.

10. Hiram Martin Chittenden, *The Yellowstone National Park: Historical and Descriptive* (Cincinnati: Robert Clark, 1895), 138.

11. Quoted in Kiki Leigh Rydell and Mary Shivers Culpin, *Managing the Matchless Wonders: A History of Administrative Development in Yellowstone National Park, 1872-1965* (Yellowstone National Park, WY: The National Park Service, 2006), 40.

12. Haines, *Yellowstone Story*, Vol. 2, 18.

13. "Territorial News," *Philipsburg (MT) Mail*, September 1, 1887, 1.

14. *St. Paul Daily Globe*, June 6, 1888, 4.

15. Harris quoted in Haines, *Yellowstone Story*, Vol. 2, 18.

16. The Stivers affair is well-documented in Haines, *Yellowstone Story*, Vol. 2, 15-18.

17. Quoted in Haines, *Yellowstone Story*, Vol. 2, 18.

18. F.A. Boutelle to Major John Pitcher, June 15, 1907, in Army Records Gardiner, MT.

19. F.A. Boutelle to Secretary of the Interior, August 17, 1890, in "Inquiry," SN-3051, 166.

20. F.A. Boutelle to Major John Pitcher, June 15, 1907.

21. Quoted in Richard A. Bartlett, *Yellowstone: A Wilderness Besieged* (Tucson: University of Arizona Press, 1988), 190.

22. Quoted in Bartlett, 170.

23. "Personal Points," *Livingston (MT) Enterprise*, February 9, 1889, 4.

24. Barbara H. Dittl and Joan Mallmann, "Plain to Fancy: The Lake Hotel, 1889-1929," *Montana: The Magazine of Western History*, Spring 1984, 40.

25. Assistant Superintendent D.W. Weimer to Superintendent David Wear, July 18, 1885, in Yellowstone Archives, quoted in Chris J. Magoc, *Yellowstone: The Creation and Selling of an American Landscape, 1870-1903* (Albuquerque: University of New Mexico Press, 1999), 116.

26. Kipling quoted in Schullery, *Searching for Yellowstone*,99-100.

27. Haines, *Yellowstone Story*, Vol. 2, 105 ("The passengers who alighted…"), 107 ("And so, with a pop of the whip…"), 129 (grizzly bear chained to a pole…).

28. James Clarkson, quoted in "Inquiry," SN-3051, 212.

CHAPTER 5

1. Mary Shivers Culpin, *A History of Concession Development in Yellowstone National Park, 1872-1966* (Yellowstone Center for Resources, WY: National Park Service, 2003), appendices.

2. Legh Freeman, *The Frontier Index*, 1868, quoted in John D. Varley and Paul Schullery, *Yellowstone Fishes: Ecology, History and Angling in the Park* (Mechanicsburg, PA: Stackpole, 1998), 12.

3. Quoted in Janet Chapple, *Yellowstone Treasures: The Traveler's Companion to the National Park* (Providence, RI: Granite Peak Publications, 2002), 143.

4. Potts and Russell quoted in Schullery, *Searching for Yellowstone*, 36, 38.

5. David E. Folsom, *The Folsom-Cook Exploration of the Upper Yellowstone in the Year 1869* (St. Paul, MN: H. L. Collins, 1894), 20.

6. Gustavus C. Doane, *The Report of Lieut. Gustavus C. Doane Upon the So-Called Yellowstone Expedition of 1870 to the Secretary of War*, as included in Louis C. Cramton, *Early History of Yellowstone National Park and Its Relation to National Park Policies* (Washington, DC: United States Government Printing Office, 1932), 130, Appendix M.

7. Hayden quoted in Marlene Deahl Merrill, ed., *Yellowstone and the Great West: Journals, Letters and Images from the 1871 Hayden*

Expedition (Lincoln: University of Nebraska Press, 1999), 152-4.

8. John L. Stoddard, *John L. Stoddard's Lectures: Southern California, Grand Canon of the Colorado River, Yellowstone National Park* (Boston: Balch Brothers, 1898), 278.

9. Nathaniel Pitt Langford, *The Discovery of Yellowstone Park* (Lincoln: University of Nebraska Press, 1972), 96-97.

10. Hiram Martin Chittenden, *The Yellowstone National Park: Historical and Descriptive* (Cincinnati: Stewart & Kidd, 1915), 340.

11. "Yellowstone Park," *Salt Lake (UT) Daily Herald*, Jan. 21, 1883, 1.

12. E. C. Waters, in testimony to the Senate Committee on Territories of the United States, March 31, 1892, as quoted in "Inquiry into the Management and Control of the Yellowstone National Park," 52nd Congress, House of Representatives, 1st Session, Report No. 1956 (Washington, DC: Government Printing Office), 53, 55. United States Congressional Serial Set, Issue 3051, Google Books ed., accessed via University of California, Davis Library.

13. Charles Gibson to Interior Secretary John Noble, March 25, 1889, quoted in "Inquiry," 55.

14. Scott McGinnis, *A Directory of Old Boats: Lake Minnetonka's Historic Steamboats, Sailboats and Launches* (Chaska, MN: S.D. McGinnis, 2010), 250-251.

15. Charles A. Zimmerman, commodore of the Lake Minnetonka Navigation Company, in a letter to his boss, James J. Hill, as quoted in McGinnis, *Old Boats*, 251.

16. McGinnis, *Old Boats*, 250-251. Although there are several mentions in historical records that that the boat sank in Lake Minnetonka and was salvaged before coming to Yellowstone, there is no actual account of the sinking, according to historian and author Scott McGinnis. McGinnis to Mike Stark, email, January 5, 2012.

17. Charles Gibson letter to Capt. F.A. Boutelle, January 6, 1890, as quoted in "Inquiry," SN-3051, 56.

18. The early conditions in Yellowstone, including details of the boat's route and Golden Gate, are thoroughly documented in Reau Campbell, *Campbell's New Revised Complete Guide to Yellowstone*

Park (Chicago: Rogers and Smith, 1909).

19. Campbell, *Campbell's New Revised Complete Guide,* 102; "The New Boat Launched," *Wonderland* (Gardiner, MT), September 21, 1905, 1.

20. John L. Stoddard, *Lectures,* 274-77.

21. Information on Amos Shaw found in Helen Fitzgerald Sanders, *A History of Montana,* Volume III (Chicago: Lewis Publishing, 1913), 1457.

22. James E. Bradford, Matthew A. Russell, Larry E. Murphy, and Timothy G. Smith, *Yellowstone National Park: Submerged Resources Survey* (Santa Fe, NM: Submerged Resources Center, Intermountain Region, National Park Service, 2003), 68-72.

23. "*Zillah* All Right," *St. Paul (MN) Daily Globe,* July 19, 1892, 2.

24. Haines, *The Yellowstone Story,* Vol. 2, 47.

25. Statement of Captain F.A. Boutelle, July 8, 1890, as referenced in "Inquiry," SN-3051, 165.

26. G.L. Henderson to Northern Pacific Railway President Thomas Oakes, July 21, 1890, and telegram from Thomas Oakes to E. C. Waters, July 23, 1890, both in "Inquiry," SN-3051, 164.

27. T.F. Oakes in letter to President's Office, Northern Pacific Railway Company, July 21, 1890, as referenced in "Inquiry," SN-3051, 165.

28. Testimony of G.L. Henderson before the subcommittee of the Committee on Public Lands, May 12, 1892, as referenced in "Inquiry," SN-3051, 204.

29. Haines, *Yellowstone Story* 2, 19.

30. "Unworthy Officials," *Forest and Stream,* August 7, 1890, 1.

31. T.F. Oakes in letter to G.L. Henderson, August 4, 1890, as referenced in "Inquiry," SN-3051, 205.

32. Haines, *Yellowstone Story,* Vol. 2, 47.

33. Expulsion details are from *Livingston (MT) Enterprise,* August 23, 1890, quoted in Lee Whittlesey, "Byways, Boats, and Buildings: Yellowstone Lake in History," *Points West* magazine (Buffalo Bill Historical Center, Cody, WY), Summer 2008, 19-23.

34. Capt. F.A. Boutelle to Interior Secretary John Noble, July 25, 1890, as referenced in "Inquiry," SN-3051, 164, 165.

35. Richard A. Bartlett, *Yellowstone: A Wilderness Besieged* (Tucson: University of Arizona Press, 1988), 191.

36. Capt. F.A. Boutelle to Secretary of the Interior John W. Noble, October 16, 1890, in Army Records Gardiner, MT.

CHAPTER 6

1. *Daily Yellowstone Journal* (Miles City, MT), March 29, 1888, 3.

2. "By the Way," *Columbus (NE) Journal*, April 1, 1891, 4.

3. "Obituary," *Billings (MT) Gazette*, February 28, 1889.

4. "Wanted in Yellowstone Park," *New York Times*, March 13, 1891.

5. Yellowstone Lake Boat Company, undated "Notice to National Park travelers" and a responding telegram from W.G. Johnson to E. C. Waters, in "Inquiry," SN-3051, 60.

6. "Sloan Has Friends," *St. Paul (MN) Daily Globe*, August 13, 1891, 2; "The scalp of Mr. Sloan," *Livingston (MT) Enterprise*, August 22, 1891, 2.

7. *St. Paul (MN) Daily Globe*, "Stabbed in the Back," August 25, 1891, 8.

8. George S. Anderson quoted in James E. Bradford, Matthew A. Russell, Larry E. Murphy, and Timothy G. Smith, *Yellowstone National Park, Submerged Resources Survey* (Sante Fe, NM: Submerged Resources Center, Intermountain Region, National Park Service, 2003), 71.

9. John L. Stoddard, *John L. Stoddard's Lectures: Southern California, Grand Canon of the Colorado River, Yellowstone National Park,* (Boston, MA: Balch Brothers, 1898), 277.

10. Quoted in Elizabeth A. Watry and Lee H. Whittlesey, *Images of America: Fort Yellowstone* (Charleston, SC: Arcadia Publishing, 2012), 70.

11. "Company D's Ramble," *St. Paul (MN) Daily Globe*, Septem-

ber 4, 1892, 12.

12. Quoted in Richard A. Bartlett, *Yellowstone: A Wilderness Besieged* (Tucson: University of Arizona Press, 1985), 156.

13. Testimony of E. C. Waters to the Senate Committee on Territories, April 28, 1892 as referenced in "Inquiry," SN-3051, 112.

14. John Noble and Charles Gibson in "Inquiry," SN-3051, IV, 41, 78.

15. Charles Gibson in "Inquiry," SN-3051, 102.

16. Bartlett, *Wilderness Besieged*, 158.

17. Gibson testimony, in "Inquiry," SN-3051, 52.

18. "Fixing up a story," *Helena (MT) Independent*, May 3, 1892, 1.

19. "Scoring Prince Russell," *New York Times*, July 21, 1892, 1.

CHAPTER 7

1. Doris Kearns Goodwin, *The Bully Pulpit: Theodore Roosevelt, William Howard Taft, and the Golden Age of Journalism* (New York: Simon & Schuster, 2013), 159.

2. Aubrey L. Haines, *The Yellowstone Story*, Vol. 2 (Boulder: Yellowstone Library and Museum Association and Colorado Associated University Press, 1977), 478.

3. Quoted in James E. Bradford, Matthew A. Russell, Larry E. Murphy, and Timothy G. Smith, Yellowstone National Park: Submerged Resources Survey (Sante Fe, NM: Submerged Resources Center, Intermountain Region, National Park Service, 2003), 71.

4. E. C. Waters to Yellowstone superintendent, details of *Zillah's* passengers, November 4, 1894, Army Records.

5. E.B. Rapley, Aug. 19, 1893, Army Records.

6. Capt. George Anderson to Interior Department about poaching arrest of William Boardman, Oct. 11, 1893, Army Records.

7. Bradford, et al., *Submerged Resources Survey*, 71.

8. "Riding in the Park," *Morning Call* (San Francisco, CA), June 13, 1893, 1.

9. The plight of Yellowstone's bison is thoroughly covered in

Margaret Mary Meagher, "The Bison of Yellowstone National Park" (National Park Service, Scientific Monograph Series, No. 1, 1973).

10. E. C. Waters to Superintendent Anderson, November 14, 1894, in Army Records.

11. Mark Rosenthal, Carol Tauber, and Edward Uhlir, *The Ark in the Park: The Story of Lincoln Park Zoo* (Chicago: The Board of Trustees of the University of Illinois, 2003), 23.

12. Haines, *Yellowstone Story*, Vol. 2, 71.

13. "Buffalo Killed at Fond Du Lac," *Copper Country Evening News* (Calumet, MI), February 8, 1897, 1.

14. Charles Lee to Superintendent Anderson, July 9, 1896, in Army Records.

15. Haines, *Yellowstone Story*, Vol. 2, 71.

16. "His New Attraction," *Anaconda (MT) Standard*, June 10, 1896, 1.

17. Annual Report of the Commissioner of Indian Affairs to the Secretary of the Interior, Part 1, 1899 (Washington, DC: Government Printing Office) 38, accessed via Google Books.

18. Col. Samuel Baldwin Marks Young, Report of the Acting Superintendent of the Yellowstone National Park to the Secretary of the Interior, 1897 (Washington, DC: Government Printing Office, 1897), 6, accessed via Google Books.

19. Wade Warren Thayer, "Camp and Cycle in Yellowstone Park," *Outing* 32, April 1898, 17-24.

20. *Columbus (NE) Journal*, Nov. 17, 1897, 1, reprinting a story from the *Philadelphia Record*.

21. E. C. Waters to Capt. O.J. Brown, October 5, 1899, in Army Records.

22. Haines, *Yellowstone Story* 2, 126.

23. Waters to Brown, October 5.

24. Haines, *Yellowstone Story* 2, 126.

25. Pauline K. Guthrie, "The Yellowstone Park—Graphic Description of the Wonderful Sights by Miss Guthrie," *Dubuque (IA) Herald*, August 12, 1900, 1.

CHAPTER 8

1. Aubrey L. Haines, *The Yellowstone Story*, Vol. 2 (Boulder: Yellowstone Library and Museum Association and Colorado Associated University Press, 1977), 457.

2. Owen Dowd to Capt. Oscar J. Brown at Fort Yellowstone, Army Records.

3. Correspondence between Interior Secretary Thomas Ryan and Superintendent John Pitcher, August 3, August 16, 1901, Army Records.

4. Correspondence between E. C. Waters and Superintendent John Pitcher, January 23, 1902, Army Records.

5. J.W. Zevely to Interior Secretary Ethan Hitchcock, October 15, 1901, Army Records.

6. J.H. Kane to Superintendent John Pitcher, January 24, January 30, 1902, Army Records.

7. James Breslau Botay to Patrick Roberts, Troop G, January 28, 1902, Army Records.

8. Superintendent John Pitcher to Interior Secretary, February 8, 1902, Army Records.

9. Pennsylvania State Sen. Bayard Henry to Superintendent John Pitcher, February 3, 1902, Army Records.

10. Henry W. Sprague ("a petty swindle"), June 21, 1902, Army Records.

11. "Visitor" to Superintendent John Pitcher, June 24, 1902, Army Records.

12. John F. Phillips to Assistant Secretary of Interior Thomas Ryan Aug. 1, 1902, Army Records.

13. W.S. Rossington to Assistant Secretary of Interior Thomas Ryan, July 26, 1902, Army Records.

14. E. C. Waters to Superintendent John Pitcher, June 29, 1902, Army Records.

15. W. F. Scott to Superintendent Pitcher, Aug. 21, 1902, Army Records.

16. Assistant Interior Secretary Ryan to "The Acting Superin-

tendent of the Yellowstone National Park," July 31, 1902, Army Records.

17. Superintendent Pitcher to E. C. Waters. August 10, 1902, Army Records.

18. Superintendent Pitcher to E. C. Waters. August 18, 1902, Army Records.

19. Handwritten letter from 1st lieutenant, 13th Cavalry at Lake Station [name indecipherable] to "The Acting Superintendent," August 8, 1902, Army Records.

20. E. C. Waters to Superintendent Pitcher, August 21, 1902, Army Records.

21. For an example, see *Ranche and Range* (Yakima, WA), January 11, 1900, 13.

22. E. C. Waters to Interior secretary and Superintendent Pitcher, August 20, 1902, Army Records.

23. Mellen quoted in Haines, *Yellowstone Story*, Vol. 2, 49.

CHAPTER 9

1. "Wants Modern Transportation," *Wonderland* (Gardiner, MT), September 3, 1903, 1.

2. Hester Ferguson Henshall's Journal, "A Trip Through Yellowstone National Park," 1903, Montana Historical Society Archives, as quoted in: M. Mark Miller, *The Stories of Yellowstone: Adventure Tales from the World's First National Park* (Rowman & Littlefield, 2014), 146-47.

3. Aubrey L. Haines, *The Yellowstone Story*, Vol. 2 (Boulder: Yellowstone Library and Museum Association and Colorado Associated University Press, 1977), 127.

4. Roosevelt, quoted in Jeremy Johnston, "Theodore Roosevelt's Quest for Wilderness: A Comparison of Roosevelt's Visits to Yellowstone and Africa," in *Beyond the Arch: Community and Conservation in Greater Yellowstone and East Africa, Proceedings of the 7th Biennial Scientific Conference on the Greater Yellowstone Ecosystem* (Yellowstone Center for Resources, Yellowstone National Park, 2004).

5. Lee H. Whittlesey and Paul Schullery, "The Roosevelt Arch: A

Centennial History of an American Icon," *Yellowstone Science*, Summer 2003, 2-18.

6. *Wonderland* (Gardiner, MT), April 30, 1903, 2.

7. Information on Harry Child in Yellowstone from Richard A. Bartlett, *Yellowstone: A Wilderness Besieged* (Tucson: University of Arizona Press, 1988), 174.

8. Harry Child to Secretary of the Interior, Jan. 21, 1902, Army Records.

9. Harry Child to Superintendent Pitcher, June 5, 1903, Army Records.

10. Superintendent Pitcher to the Secretary of the Interior, June 6, 1903, Army Records.

11. Bartlett, 187-188.

12. W.W. Wylie to Superintendent Pitcher, Nov. 21, 1903, Army Records.

13. Mrs. O.J. de Lendercie to Yellowstone superintendent, June 14, 1903, Army records.

14. E. C. Waters, *Explanation and Argument of The Yellowstone Lake Boat Co.* (Ripon, WI: E. L. Howe, printer, 1903), Army Records.

15. Benjamin B. Odell Jr. to President Theodore Roosevelt, November 28, 1903, in Theodore Roosevelt Papers, Library of Congress Manuscript Division, and Theodore Roosevelt Digital Library, Dickinson State University, ND, http://www.theodorerooseveltcenter.org/Research/Digital-Library/Record/ImageViewer.aspx?libID=o186594

16. Roosevelt to Odell, December 1, 1903, Roosevelt Papers, Library of Congress Manuscripts division, and Theodore Roosevelt Digital Library, Dickinson State.

17. Wonderland, September 24, 1903.

18. *Wonderland* (Gardiner, MT), October 10, 1903.

19. "New Steamer in Yellowstone," *Minneapolis (MN) Journal*, November 17, 1903, 3.

20. W.W. Wylie to Superintendent Pitcher, Nov. 21, 1903, Army Records.

CHAPTER 10

1. James Fullerton, *Autobiography of Roosevelt's Adversary* (Boston: Roxburgh Publishing, 1912), 121.

2. "Yellowstone Park Scandal," *New York Times*, December 1, 1903, 9.

3. Fullerton, *Autobiography*.

4. James Fullerton, Sportsman Game Protective Association, to U.S. Representative John Lacey, February 9, 1904, and response from Superintendent Pitcher to Rep. Lacey on March 9, 1904, Army Records.

5. Fullerton, *Autobiography*, 131.

6. Telegram, Superintendent Pitcher to E. C. Waters, July 23, 1904, and response by Waters on July 24, 1904, Army Records.

7. Harry Child to Superintendent Pitcher, July 22, 1904, plus responses on August 15 and August 22, 1904, plus telegram from E. C. Waters to Pitcher, July 2, 1904, Army Records.

8. Letters among Harry Child, July 22, 1904, archive document 5513, and F. Jay Haynes, July 24, 1904, and Superintendent Pitcher, July 25, 1904, Army Records.

9. Telegram and response, E. C. Waters to Superintendent Pitcher, July 21-22, 1904, and archive document 5515, Army Records.

10. E. C. Waters to Superintendent Pitcher, August 14, 1904, Army Records.

11. Unsigned letter, from official at Thumb Station to Superintendent Pitcher, August 17, 1904, Army Records.

12. Waters to Pitcher, August 14, 1904, Army Records.

13. Superintendent Pitcher to Interior secretary, October 5, 1904, Army Records. 14. "New Steamer for the Park," *Minneapolis Journal*, December 13, 1904, 11.

CHAPTER 11

1. "News of Death is Great Shock," *Daily Commonwealth* (Fond du Lac, WI); January 6, 1905; *Daily Reporter* (Milwaukee), "Was

Tired of Living," January 7, 1905.

2. E. C. Waters to undisclosed recipients, January 18, 1905, Army Records.

3. E. C. Waters to Superintendent Pitcher, July 7, 1905, with response by Harry Child on July 12, 1905, Army Records.

4. "Outlook Good for This Year," *Wonderland* (Gardiner, MT), January 14, 1905, 1.

5. "A Steam Yacht on Yellowstone Lake," *Marine Engineering*, Vol. 10, December 1905, 520.

6. James E. Bradford, Matthew A. Russell, Larry E. Murphy, and Timothy G. Smith, *Yellowstone National Park, Submerged Resources Survey* (Sante Fe, NM: Submerged Resources Center, Intermountain Region, National Park Service, 2003), 143.

7. Bradford, et al., *Submerged Resources Survey*, 143.

8. Yellowstone Historian Aubrey Haines to David Hashley, February 16, 1962, Yellowstone National Park Archives.

9. The christening ceremony is detailed in "The New Boat Launched," *Wonderland*, September 21, 1905, 1.

CHAPTER 12

1. E. C. Waters to Superintendent John Pitcher, with additional correspondence from Secretary of Interior Ethan Hitchcock, July 2, 1906, Army Records.

2. Elmer J. Whiteley to Superintendent Pitcher, August 11, 1906, Army Records.

3. "Hotel Clerk Wins Young Heiress," *San Francisco Call*, September 28, 1906, 3.

4. E. C. Waters to Secretary of the Interior, September 30, 1906, Army Records.

5. Unsigned and undated memo "concerning Mr. Dave Edwards, winter keeper for the Yellowstone Lake Boat Company, who died at Lake Outlet, November 12, 1906," Army Records.

6. Yellowstone superintendent to E. C. Waters about Edwards' burial location, November 21, 1906, Army Records.

7. Sgt. Arthur Franson to commanding officer, Fort Yellowstone, about skull found on Stevenson Island, June 27, 1907, archive document 7023, Army Records.

8. The "paved over for a gas station" story is told in Lee H. Whittlesey, *Death in Yellowstone: Accidents and Foolhardiness in the First National Park* (Lanham, MD: Roberts Rinehart, 1995), 217; reprint, 2014, 311.

9. E. C. Waters to Rep. Bourke Cockran, February 25, 1907, Army Records.

10. Bourke Cockran to President Theodore Roosevelt, June 5, 1907, Army Records.

11. E. C. Waters to Bourke Cockran, February 25, 1907, Army Records.

12. Interior Secretary James Garfield to Yellowstone Lake Boat Company, March 12, 1907, archive document 6326, Army Records.

13. Letter (and related correspondence) from E. C. Waters to Bourke Cockran, May 28, 1907, Army Records.

14. Bourke Cockran to President Theodore Roosevelt, June 5, 1907, Army Records.

15. President Theodore Roosevelt to Bourke Cockran and memo from Roosevelt's secretary to Superintendent "General" Young, June 6, 1907, Army Records.

16. F.W. Vowinnkel, M.D., to Lieutenant-General S.M.B. Young, June 12, 1907, Army Records.

17. Capt. M.O. Bigelow, 6th Cavalry, to Lieut. Gen. S.B.M. Young, June 13, 1907, Army records.

18. Unsigned memo from captain of 8th Cavalry to Lieut. General S.B.M. Young, June 21, 1907, Army Records.

CHAPTER 13

1. Nathaniel Pitt Langford, *The Discovery of Yellowstone Park* (Lincoln: University of Nebraska Press, 1972), 54.

2. William Thomas to General S.B.M. Young, July 2, 1907, Army Records.

3. Transcription of "Statement from Jerome Chapin, Esq., of Battle Creek, Michigan With Reference to Conduct on Drunken Soldier on Board the Steamer E. C. Waters on Yellowstone Lake, July 23, 1907," archive document 7001, Army Records.

4. F.A. Boutelle to Major John Pitcher, June 15, 1907, Army Records.

5. Telegram to Superintendent Young from Adjt. General Ainsworth, June 15, 1907, about Waters' service in the Civil War, Army Records.

6. W.H. Talmage Co. to Yellowstone official, June 27, 1907, Army Records.

7. A.L. Babcock, president of the Yellowstone National Bank, to Superintendent Pitcher, June 28, 1907, Army Records.

8. Unsigned memo, referencing "information received thro' Mr. Pryor, Cashier Bank at Gardiner, that Yegen Bros. of Billings, Mont., hold note against Waters for about $3,500…"), July 3, 1907, Army Records.

9. Unsigned memo, referencing "information given by Mr. C.N. Sargent, sec'y and treas. of the W.A. Hall Co., of Gardiner, Mont. concerning Mr. E. C. Waters…"), June 27, 1907, Army Records.

10. "Sues for Large Sum," *Billings (MT) Gazette*, December 8, 1905, 3.

11. Superintendent Young to E. C. Waters, August 2, 1907, Army Records.

12. William Scott to Gen. S.B.M. Young, August 24, 1907, Army Records.

13. T.S. Palmer to Gen. S.B.M. Young, August 19, 1907, Army Records.

14. Young to Waters, August 2, 1907.

15. E. C. Waters to John D. Sloan, August 6, 1907, archive document 6240, Army Records.

16. "Taft Now at Yellowstone," *Seattle Star*, September 2, 1907, 7.

17. President William H. Taft to Interior Secretary Richard A. Ballinger, June 3, 1909, Richard A. Ballinger Papers, Manuscript

Collection 0015, University Libraries, University of Washington, Seattle.

18. Samuel Baldwin Marks Young, *Annual Report of the Superintendent of the Yellowstone National Park to the Secretary of the Interior* (Washington, DC: Government Printing Office, 1907), 5-6.

19. Bartlett, *Wilderness Besieged*, 193.

20. E. C. Waters, "Temporary Offices of the Yellowstone Lake Boat Company" (with related correspondence and documents), to Interior secretary, January 10, 1908, Army Records.

21. Martha ("M.B.") Waters to Henry T. Allen, Superintendent, Yellowstone Park, Wyoming, June 22, 1908, Army Records.

22. W.D. Frost, "Tuberculosis or Consumption With Special Reference to Wisconsin Conditions," *Bulletin of the University of Wisconsin* (Madison, WI, University Extension Series), No. 319, Vol. 1, October 1909, 63.

23. Centers for Disease Control and Prevention, *Deaths and Death Rates for Leading Causes of Death: Death Registration Dates, 1900-1940*.

24. Martha "M.B." Waters to Henry T. Allen, June 22, 1908.

25. Superintendent Young to Interior Secretary, July 3, 1908, Army Records.

26. Superintendent Young to Yellowstone Lake Boat Co., June 15, 1908, Army Records.

27. Aubrey L. Haines, *The Yellowstone Story*, Vol. 2 (Boulder: Yellowstone Library and Museum Association and Colorado Associated University Press, 1977), 457.

28. "List of property belonging to E. C. Waters at Yellowstone Lake," December 30, 1908, Army Records.

29. President W.H. Taft to R.A. Ballinger, June 3, 1909, Richard A. Ballinger Papers,.

30. Arthur Vorys to Superintendent Benson, July 21, 1909, Army Records.

31. *Daily Northwestern* (Oshkosh, WI), August 7, 1909.

32. Interior Secretary Richard Ballinger to Superintendent Harry Benson, September 17, 1909, with response from Benson, Army

Records.

33. Former Superintendent Young, at the War Department, to Yellowstone Superintendent Benson, April 23, 1910, Army Records.

34. "Confidential" letter to Young, addressed "My dear General," that is unsigned, but almost certainly from Benson, April 27, 1910, Army Records.

35. Interior Secretary Ballinger to President William H. Taft, May 31, 1910, Richard A. Ballinger Papers.

36. Telegram, E. C. Waters to Superintendent Benson, July 7, 1910, Army Records.

37. Superintendent Benson to Interior Secretary, October 25, 1910, Army Records.

38. Interior Secretary Richard Ballinger to President William H. Taft, May 31, 1910, Richard A. Ballinger Papers.

CHAPTER 14

1. Richard A. Bartlett, *Yellowstone: A Wilderness Besieged* (Tucson: University of Arizona Press, 1988), 193.

2. *Zillah* details from James E. Bradford, Matthew A. Russell, Larry E. Murphy, and Timothy G. Smith, *Yellowstone National Park: Submerged Resources Survey* (Santa Fe, NM: Submerged Resources Center, Intermountain Region, National Park Service, 2003), 73.

3. The steamboat *E. C. Waters'* later years from Aubrey L. Haines, *The Yellowstone Story*, Vol. 2 (Boulder: Yellowstone Library and Museum Association and Colorado Associated University Press, 1977), 316.

4. Jack Croney to W.M. Nichols, May 23, 1931, Yellowstone National Park Archives (YNP Archives), Gardiner, MT.

5. E.E. Ogston to Chief Ranger George Baggley, June 5, 1931, YNP Archives, Gardiner, MT.

6. Bradford, et al., *Submerged Resources Survey*, 72-78.

7. Jack Croney to W.M. Nichols, May 23, 1931, YNP Archives.

8. Guy D. Edwards to Mr. W.M. Nichols, president, Yellowstone Park Boat Co., June 11, 1931, YNP Archives.

9. Haines, *Yellowstone Story*, Vol. 2, 316.

10. E.E. Ogston to Chief Ranger George Baggley, June 5, 1931, YNP Archives.

11. "Ela C. Waters Is Dead At Waupaca, Funeral in Fondy," *Daily Commonwealth* (Fond du Lac, WI), August 18, 1926.

12. Horace Albright to Commanding Officer, Old Soldiers Home, Fond du Lac, Wisconsin, October 28, 1926, YNP Archives.

EPILOGUE

1. James E. Bradford, Matthew A. Russell, Larry E. Murphy, and Timothy G. Smith, *Yellowstone National Park: Submerged Resources Survey* (Santa Fe, NM: Submerged Resources Center, Intermountain Region, National Park Service, 2003), 73.

ABOUT THE AUTHOR

Mike Stark spent more than fifteen years covering the American West as a journalist for newspapers and the Associated Press, including six years writing about Yellowstone National Park. He lives in Tucson, Arizona, with his wife and daughter.

ACKNOWLEDGEMENTS

Written history is borne of the things left behind and cared for by others, so I'm deeply indebted to those who have preserved Yellowstone's history with such concern, including staff at the Yellowstone Heritage and Research Center. The preservation and organization of the park's documents—including handwritten notes, telegrams, letters and reports—was invaluable for this project. I'm grateful to those who pointed me in the right direction and were patient with my requests. Yellowstone has a long and storied legion of historians and writers who have told the story of the place, including Aubrey Haines, Hiram Chittenden, Horace Albright, Richard Bartlett, Chris J. Magoc, Paul Schullery and Lee Whittlesey. I am indebted to them all. I'm especially thankful for my conversations with Lee Whittlesey, the park's current historian, who did his best to transform my journalist's eye into a historian's, and to remind me of this work's responsibility to those who will come after us in their own pursuit to tell Yellowstone's story. Any mistakes in this work are solely my own.

A deep thanks too to the National Park Service's Submerged Resources Center, who recognized the importance of the wreck of the *E. C. Waters* and conducted such a thorough examination of its history and configuration on the shore of Stevenson Island.

This work would also not have been possible without those who wrote some of the first drafts of this history, people like Helen Fitzgerald Sanders, who wrote an exhaustive history of Montana (including a biographical sketch of E. C. Waters) in the early 1900s, and Maurice McKenna, who wrote his own exhaustive book on the history of Wisconsin's Fond du Lac County. Since the beginning, Yellowstone has always drawn the attention of journalists, writers and curiosity-seekers compelled to tell the world about what they've seen. I was among them for many years as a reporter at *The Billings Gazette* in Montana, and had the lucky privilege every day to work with my editor Tom Tollefson, whose penciled notes on my stories always made them better and made me smarter. Tom also looked at an early draft of this manuscript and provided some much-needed ideas for improvements, as did my wife Karen Mockler, and friend, Andy Parker.

There are too many other friends, historians, fellow writers and Yellowstone enthusiasts to name here but rest assured the list is long. Finally a heartfelt thanks to my wife, Karen, and daughter, Birdie, who put up with this obsession for many years, including my writing binges, boxes of documents, books and endless stacks of pawed-over papers. Yellowstone remains one of our most favorite places on the planet.